WEATHER

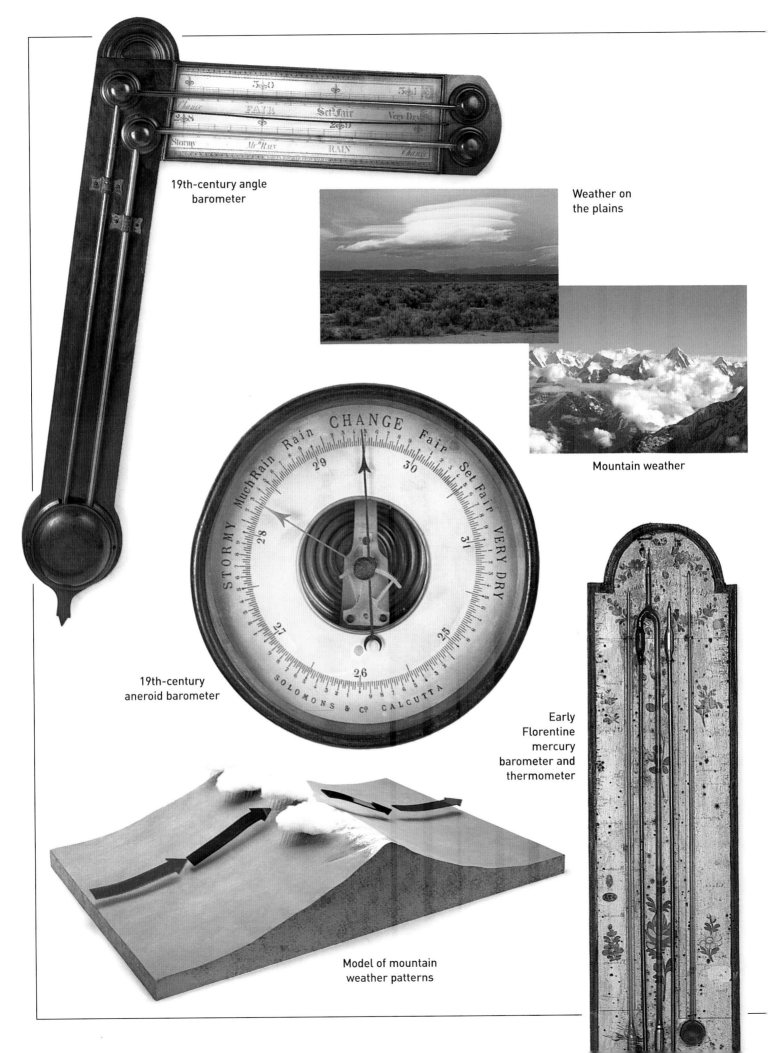

19th-century angle
barometer

Weather on
the plains

Mountain weather

19th-century
aneroid barometer

Early
Florentine
mercury
barometer and
thermometer

Model of mountain
weather patterns

Snow crystal

EYEWITNESS
WEATHER

Pocket hygrometer

Weather vane

Early English
thermometer

Model of a cold front

DK

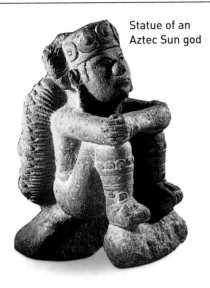

Statue of an
Aztec Sun god

Shut pinecone
signals
wet weather

Open pine
cone signals
dry weather

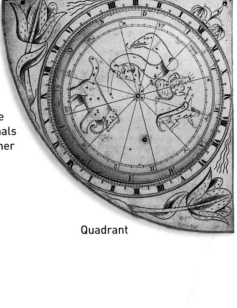

Quadrant

DK | Penguin
Random
House

Project editors John Farndon, Marion Dent
Art editor Alison Anholt-White
Senior editor Helen Parker
Senior art editors Jacquie Gulliver, Julia Harris
Production Louise Barratt
Picture research Diana Morris
Special photography Karl Shone, Keith Percival
Editorial consultant Jim Sharp

RELAUNCH EDITION

DK UK
Senior editor Francesca Baines
Senior art editor Spencer Holbrook
US senior editor Margaret Parrish
Jacket coordinator Claire Gell
Jacket designer Natalie Godwin
Jacket design development manager Sophia MTT
Producer, pre-production Jacqueline Street
Producer Vivienne Yong
Managing art editor Philip Letsu
Publisher Andrew Macintyre
Associate publishing director Liz Wheeler
Design director Stuart Jackman
Publishing director Jonathan Metcalf

DK INDIA
Assistant editor Ateendriya Gupta
Art editor Alpana Aditya
DTP designer Pawan Kumar
Senior DTP designer Harish Aggarwal
Picture researcher Sakshi Saluja
Jacket designer Dhirendra Singh
Managing jackets editor Saloni Singh
Pre-production manager Balwant Singh
Managing editor Kingshuk Ghoshal
Managing art editor Govind Mittal

First American Edition, 1991
This edition published in the United States in 2016 by
DK Publishing, 345 Hudson Street, New York, New York 10014

Copyright © 1991, 2002, 2007, 2016 Dorling Kindersley Limited
DK, a Division of Penguin Random House LLC

16 17 18 19 20 10 9 8 7 6 5 4 3 2 1
001—294904—Jun/16

Published in Great Britain by Dorling Kindersley Limited.

A catalog record for this book is available from the Library of Congress.

ISBN: 978-1-4654-5180-4 (Paperback)
ISBN: 978-1-4654-5181-1 (ALB)

DK books are available at special discounts when purchased in bulk
for sales promotions, premiums, fund-raising, or educational use.
For details, contact: DK Publishing Special Markets,
345 Hudson Street, New York, New York 10014
SpecialSales@dk.com

Printed and bound in China

A WORLD OF IDEAS:
SEE ALL THERE IS TO KNOW

www.dk.com

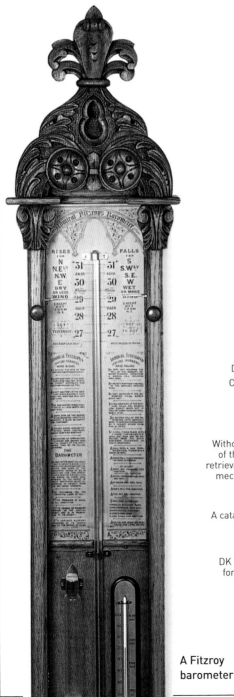

A Fitzroy
barometer

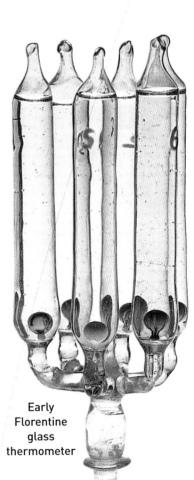

Early
Florentine
glass
thermometer

Contents

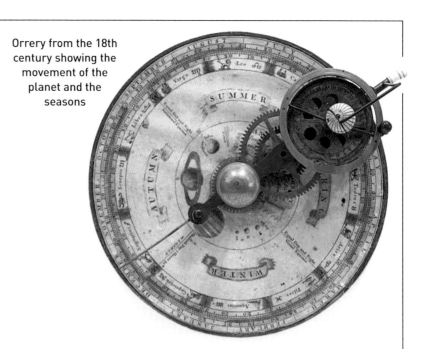

Orrery from the 18th century showing the movement of the planet and the seasons

The restless air

Our planet is surrounded by a blanket of gases called the atmosphere. These gases protect us from the intense heat of the Sun in the day and the freezing temperatures of night. The very lowest 6 miles (10 km) of the atmosphere—the air in which we live and breathe—is known as the troposphere. This layer of air is forever on the move, boiling and bubbling in the Sun's heat. It is the constant swirling of the troposphere that gives us our weather, from the warm, still days of summer to the wildest storms of winter.

Taking the air
In the 19th century, scientists in hot-air balloons found that the air got colder the higher they went. Unmanned balloons later proved that air gets colder only up to a certain point—the tropopause, or the top of the troposphere.

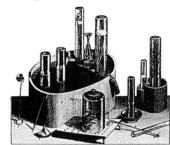

Breath for life
In the 1770s, scientist Joseph Priestley found that air contained an unknown vital ingredient needed by animals to survive.

Planet of clouds
In photographs from space, great swirls of cloud can be seen over Earth. Along the equator is a long ribbon of cloud, formed by the intense heat of the Sun stirring up rising currents of air. These carry moisture from the ocean so high into the air that it cools and turns into water droplets, forming clouds.

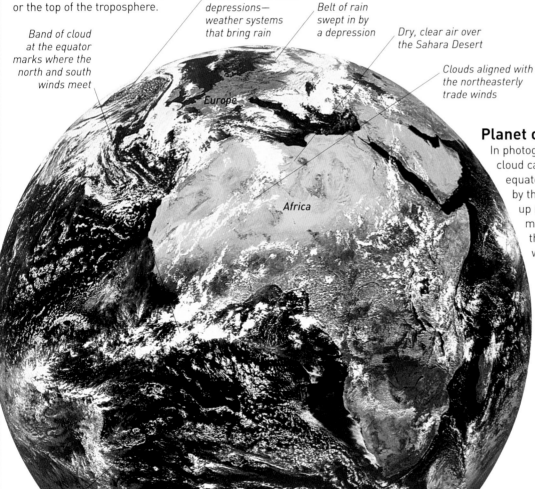

Whirls of cloud show depressions— weather systems that bring rain

Belt of rain swept in by a depression

Dry, clear air over the Sahara Desert

Clouds aligned with the northeasterly trade winds

Band of cloud at the equator marks where the north and south winds meet

Europe

Africa

Atlantic Ocean

Zone where unpredictable westerly winds blow

Whirls of cloud around mid-latitude depressions

What is air?
In the 1780s, French chemist Antoine Lavoisier discovered that air contained three main gases: oxygen, nitrogen, and carbon dioxide.

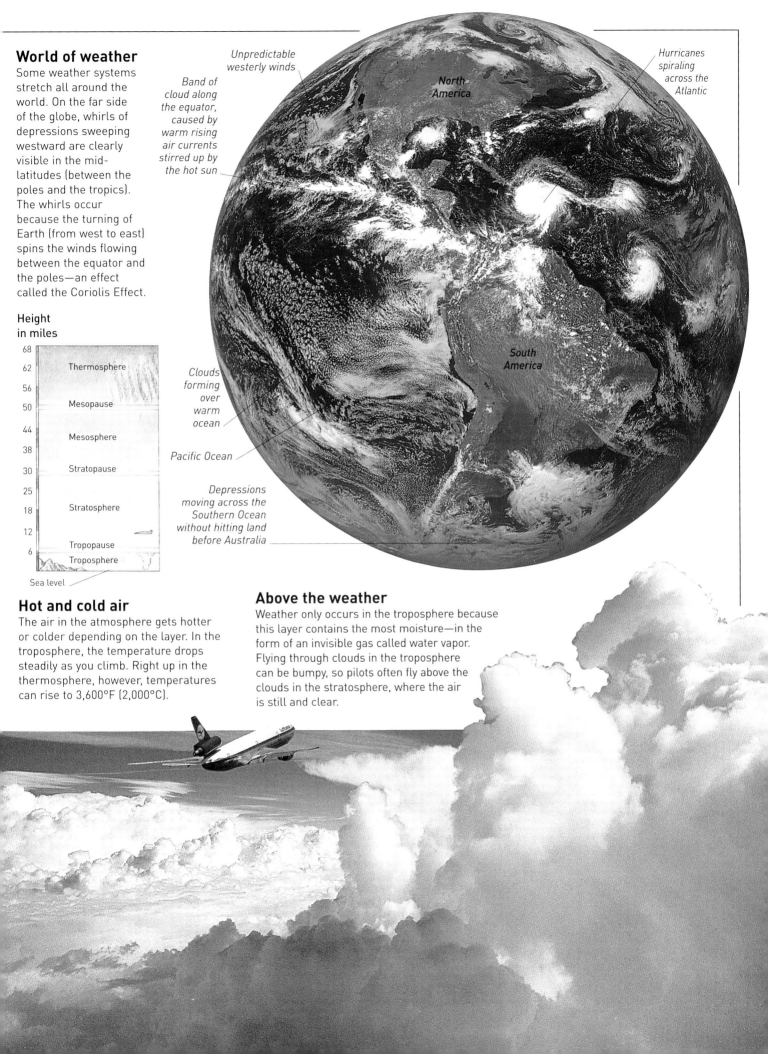

World of weather

Some weather systems stretch all around the world. On the far side of the globe, whirls of depressions sweeping westward are clearly visible in the mid-latitudes (between the poles and the tropics). The whirls occur because the turning of Earth (from west to east) spins the winds flowing between the equator and the poles—an effect called the Coriolis Effect.

Height in miles

68	
62	Thermosphere
56	
50	Mesopause
44	Mesosphere
38	
30	Stratopause
25	
18	Stratosphere
12	
6	Tropopause
	Troposphere

Sea level

Unpredictable westerly winds

Band of cloud along the equator, caused by warm rising air currents stirred up by the hot sun

North America

Hurricanes spiraling across the Atlantic

Clouds forming over warm ocean

Pacific Ocean

South America

Depressions moving across the Southern Ocean without hitting land before Australia

Hot and cold air

The air in the atmosphere gets hotter or colder depending on the layer. In the troposphere, the temperature drops steadily as you climb. Right up in the thermosphere, however, temperatures can rise to 3,600°F (2,000°C).

Above the weather

Weather only occurs in the troposphere because this layer contains the most moisture—in the form of an invisible gas called water vapor. Flying through clouds in the troposphere can be bumpy, so pilots often fly above the clouds in the stratosphere, where the air is still and clear.

Natural signs

Sailors, farmers, and others whose livelihood depends on the weather learned long ago that the natural world can provide useful clues about the weather to come. Many of these natural signs are based on superstition. But tiny variations in the air, which we cannot feel, often affect plants and animals. A change in their appearance or behavior may be a sign of a change in the weather.

People such as travelers and sailors had to be aware of the weather at all times.

Sun day opening
The scarlet pimpernel has long been used to predict the weather. Its tiny flowers open wide in sunny weather, but close up tightly when rain is in the air.

Groundhog Day
In the US, February 2 is Groundhog Day. It is said that if a groundhog's shadow appears at noon, it will be cold for the next six weeks.

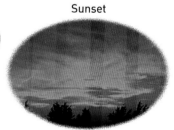

Sunset

Sunrise

Seeing red
According to tradition, a red sunset means that clear weather will follow, while a red sunrise means that storms are on the way.

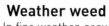

Weather weed
In fine weather, seaweed shrivels and becomes dry. If rain threatens, the weed swells and feels damp.

Curly warning
Wool reacts to moisture in the air. When the air is dry, it shrinks and curls up. If rain is due, the wool swells and straightens out.

Cricket forecast
Grasshoppers are sensitive to changes in the weather, chirruping louder and louder as the temperature rises. The chirruping sound is made by their hind legs rubbing against their hard front wings.

Wet

Dry

Weather cones
A pinecone is one of the most reliable natural weather predictors. In dry weather, the scales on the cone shrivel up and open out. When rain is on the way, the scales shut tightly.

Oak

Ash

Glorious morning
Like the scarlet pimpernel, the petals of morning glory open and shut in response to the weather. These wide-open blooms indicate good weather.

Soak or splash?
An old English saying states: *If the oak flowers before the ash, we shall have a splash* (meaning only light rain for the next month or so). *If the ash flowers before the oak, we shall have a soak* (meaning very wet weather). There is, however, no evidence to support this prediction.

Lying cows
People sometimes say that if cows are lying down, then rain must be on the way. While many animals can sense changes in the weather, this prediction has no basis in fact.

Spring is here
The blooming of white flowers on the horse chestnut tree is said to herald the end of winter. These flowers will only appear once the weather is mild enough.

Some country folks expect a severe winter if squirrels have very bushy tails, or gather big stores of nuts in the fall.

The science of weather

Weather and the atmosphere have fascinated scientists for centuries. In ancient Greece, the philosopher Aristotle studied the atmosphere and gave us the word "meteorology"—the science of weather. In 17th-century Italy, scientists developed the first instruments to measure changes in the atmosphere. In around 1600, Italian mathematician Galileo Galilei created the first thermometer. Forty years later, his assistant Torricelli developed the first barometer for measuring air pressure. The first really successful thermometer was made by German physicist Daniel Fahrenheit in about 1709.

Heat balls
The philosopher Philo proved that warm air expands in the 2nd century BCE. He joined a hollow ball to a pitcher of water and found that air bubbled through the water when the ball was heated by the Sun.

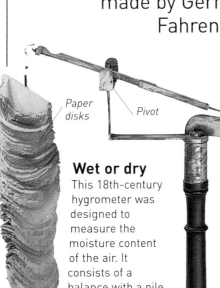

Paper disks

Pivot

Scale indicating humidity

Wet or dry
This 18th-century hygrometer was designed to measure the moisture content of the air. It consists of a balance with a pile of soft paper disks on one arm. If the air is dry, the disks dry out and weigh less. If the air is damp, they absorb water and weigh more, pulling the pointer up.

Icy water
This replica of an early hygrometer (right) has a hollow core that can be filled with ice. Moisture in the air cools and condenses (turns into water droplets) on the outside, then runs down into a measuring flask. The amount of water collected in the flask indicates the moisture content of the air.

Flask for collecting water

Galileo
Galileo believed that air had weight, or pressure, and asked his assistant Torricelli to perform experiments that would prove his theories.

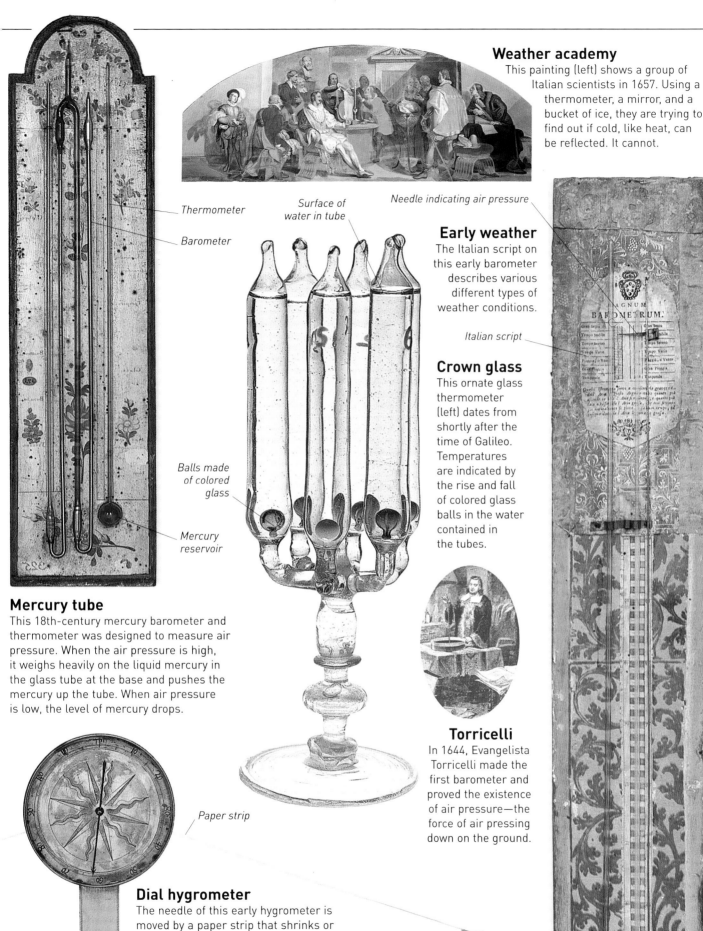

Weather academy
This painting (left) shows a group of Italian scientists in 1657. Using a thermometer, a mirror, and a bucket of ice, they are trying to find out if cold, like heat, can be reflected. It cannot.

Thermometer

Barometer

Surface of water in tube

Needle indicating air pressure

Early weather
The Italian script on this early barometer describes various different types of weather conditions.

Italian script

MAGNUM
BAROMETRUM.

Crown glass
This ornate glass thermometer (left) dates from shortly after the time of Galileo. Temperatures are indicated by the rise and fall of colored glass balls in the water contained in the tubes.

Balls made of colored glass

Mercury reservoir

Mercury tube
This 18th-century mercury barometer and thermometer was designed to measure air pressure. When the air pressure is high, it weighs heavily on the liquid mercury in the glass tube at the base and pushes the mercury up the tube. When air pressure is low, the level of mercury drops.

Torricelli
In 1644, Evangelista Torricelli made the first barometer and proved the existence of air pressure—the force of air pressing down on the ground.

Paper strip

Dial hygrometer
The needle of this early hygrometer is moved by a paper strip that shrinks or stretches in response to the dampness of the air.

Watching the weather

Meteorologists (weather scientists) gather information about the weather from a wide range of sources. A global network of weather stations constantly monitors conditions on land and at sea. Weather balloons and research aircraft are sent high into the atmosphere, while out in space, satellites circle the Earth, beaming back pictures of cloud and temperature patterns.

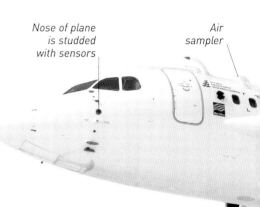

Atmospheric research aircraft

Nose of plane is studded with sensors

Air sampler

Weather forecasting networks were set up to warn ships of approaching storms.

Thermometers in ventilated white surround

Wind vane for measuring wind direction

Anemometer for measuring wind speed

Fixed station

The World Meteorological Organization has a network of about 11,000 permanent weather stations around the world. Every three hours, weather reports are sent to forecasting centers in individual countries so they can create their own weather forecasts.

Radio transmitter for sending data via satellite to base

Temperature and humidity probes inside screen

Navigation light

Anemometer

Transmitter antenna

Barometric pressure sensor

Transmitter gives buoy position to orbiting satellite

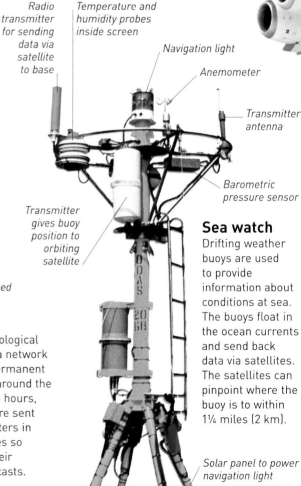

Sea watch

Drifting weather buoys are used to provide information about conditions at sea. The buoys float in the ocean currents and send back data via satellites. The satellites can pinpoint where the buoy is to within 1¼ miles (2 km).

Solar panel to power navigation light

High view

Since 1960, satellite pictures have played a vital role in monitoring the weather. There are two basic types of picture. Normal satellite photos show cloud and wind patterns, while special infrared pictures show temperatures at the nearest visible point.

"Blister" on fuselage houses monitoring equipment

Sensors mounted on under-wing pylon

Out of this world

There are two types of weather satellite. Geostationary satellites stay fixed in the same spot, about 21,500 miles (36,000 km) out in space. They provide an almost complete picture of the globe (except for the two poles) every half hour. Polar-orbiting satellites circle the Earth from pole to pole. They provide a changing, more detailed weather picture from closer to the Earth's surface.

Plane carries a crew of three and up to eighteen scientists

Flying laboratory

Weather research planes, such as this one, are equipped with highly sophisticated equipment to monitor weather and climate. The planes are designed to take a wide range of readings at different levels in the atmosphere. Some can even fly right into the eye of a hurricane to get detailed information on wind speed, air pressure, temperature, and humidity.

Onboard scientist checking data

Joseph Henry

In 1848, Joseph Henry set up a system to obtain up-to-date weather reports from across the US. By 1849, more than 200 people were sending measurements back to Mr. Henry at the Smithsonian Institute in Washington. The data was used to provide daily weather reports for the *Washington Evening Post*.

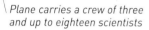

Sky probe

Twice a day, hundreds of weather balloons filled with helium gas are launched into the atmosphere across the world. Attached to each balloon is a package of instruments called a radiosonde. These instruments take humidity, temperature, and pressure readings, and radio the results back to Earth.

Balloon is tracked either by radar or with survey equipment

Tube for filling balloon with helium gas

Long line for supporting recording instruments

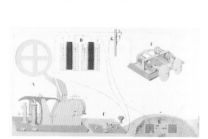

Data collection

Samuel Morse's invention of the telegraph in the 1840s meant that weather reports could be sent instantly over long distances through electric cables. Information was sent using a coded sequence of short and long pauses, known as Morse Code.

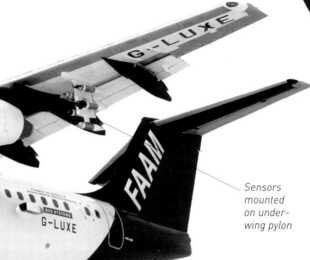

Forecasting

Every minute, weather observations taken by weather stations, ships, satellites, balloons, and radar all around the world are fed into powerful supercomputers, able to perform millions of calculations each second. Meteorologists use this information to make short-range weather forecasts for the next 24 hours and draw up a weather map, or "synoptic chart," showing air pressure, temperature, wind, cloud cover, and humidity (moisture in the air). They can also make fairly accurate long-range forecasts for up to a week.

Physicist Jean de Borda linked changes in air pressure to wind speed.

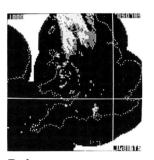

Rain scan
Radar signals reflect rain, hail, and snow. The intensity of the reflection shows how heavily rain is falling. Meteorologists use this data to create a map of rainfall intensity, as above.

Blue sky
Fair weather, with blue sky and light cloud, is often linked to high-pressure zones, or "anticyclones."

Blue triangles and red semicircles show cold fronts moving beneath warm fronts

Lines with blue triangles show a cold front, where cold air is moving toward warmer air

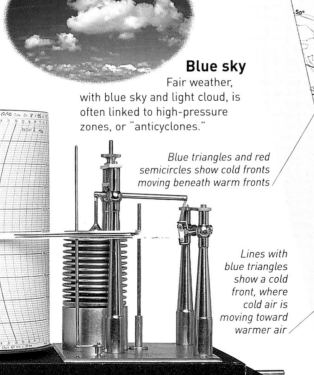

Barograph
This barograph (left) is designed to make a continuous record of changing air pressure. As the air pressure changes, the drum expands and contracts. A pen attached to the lid of the drum draws the ups and downs continuously on a rotating sheet of graph paper.

Storm by satellite

The cold front and depression, marked on the synoptic chart (below), are clearly revealed by the whirl of clouds in this satellite photograph (left).

Closely spaced isobars indicate strong wind

Low, or depression

Dull days

Wet and stormy weather is often associated with low fronts and low-pressure zones, or depressions.

Charting the weather

The most obvious features on any weather map, or synoptic chart, are the long, curved lines called isobars. These lines link points of equal air pressure, and are usually measured in millibars (mb). The inside circles linked by low-pressure isobars are depressions, where the air is rising. These frequently bring wind, clouds, and rain. The inside circles linked by high-pressure isobars are highs, where air is sinking. These usually bring dry, settled weather.

Weather stations, with observations for wind, cloud cover, and other factors (see key)

Isobar joining points of equal air pressure

Lines with red semicircles show a warm front, where warm air is pushing over cold air

Richardson

In the 1920s, Lewis Richardson devised "numeric weather predictions." He believed that the key to weather forecasting was to observe weather conditions at evenly spaced points across the world at the same time. Richardson tried with this specially built calculator but the calculations were too huge. Numeric forecasting has only become possible with the development of supercomputers.

Key to symbols

Temperature: 45°F (7°C)

Current weather: heavy rain

Visibility: 1.5 miles (2.5 km)

Dew point: 43°F (6°C)

Stratus cloud

Cloud cover complete

07   180

25 ∴

27

06

‑ ‑ ‑

8/12

Air pressure: 1018 mb

Moderate, north-easterly wind

Pressure fallen by 2.7 mb in last 3 hours

Rain in past hour

Cloud base height (1,310 ft/400 m)

The Sun

A close-up view of the Sun showing a violent storm erupting at the surface.

Weather happens because the Sun's heat keeps the atmosphere in constant motion. But the Sun's power to heat the air varies—across the world, through the day, and through the year. All these variations depend on the Sun's height in the sky. When the Sun is high in the sky, its rays strike the ground directly, giving maximum heat. When it is low, the rays strike the ground at an angle, spreading the heat over a wider area.

18th-century carved ivory pocket sundial

Gnomon

Daily rhythms

The shadow cast by the needle, or "gnomon," of a sundial (left and above), shifts as the Sun moves through the sky from sunrise to sunset, indicating the time of day.

18th-century brass sundial

Hot spots

Deserts occur wherever the air is very dry, so few clouds can form. They can be hot, such as the Sahara, or cold, such as the Gobi in central Asia.

- Mountain
- Cold plain
- Polar

- Temperate
- Mediterranean
- Warm plain
- Subtropical
- Tropical
- Desert

Polar cold

Vast areas of the Arctic and Antarctic are covered in a permanent sheet of ice.

The world's climates

As Earth's surface is curved, the Sun's rays strike different parts at different angles, dividing the world into distinct climate zones. Climate is the average weather experienced in a particular place over a period of time. The hottest places are the tropics along the equator, where the Sun is almost overhead at noon. The coldest places are the poles, where the Sun's rays are spread over a wide area. In between these extremes lie the temperate zones.

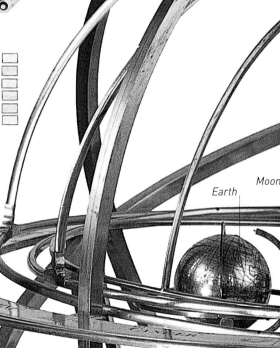

Earth

Moon

Seasoned weather

In the tropics, there are often just two seasons in the year, one wet and one dry. In hot deserts, there are no real seasons, as the weather changes little through the year. But in the temperate zones, the weather passes through four distinct phases during the year: spring, summer, fall, and winter.

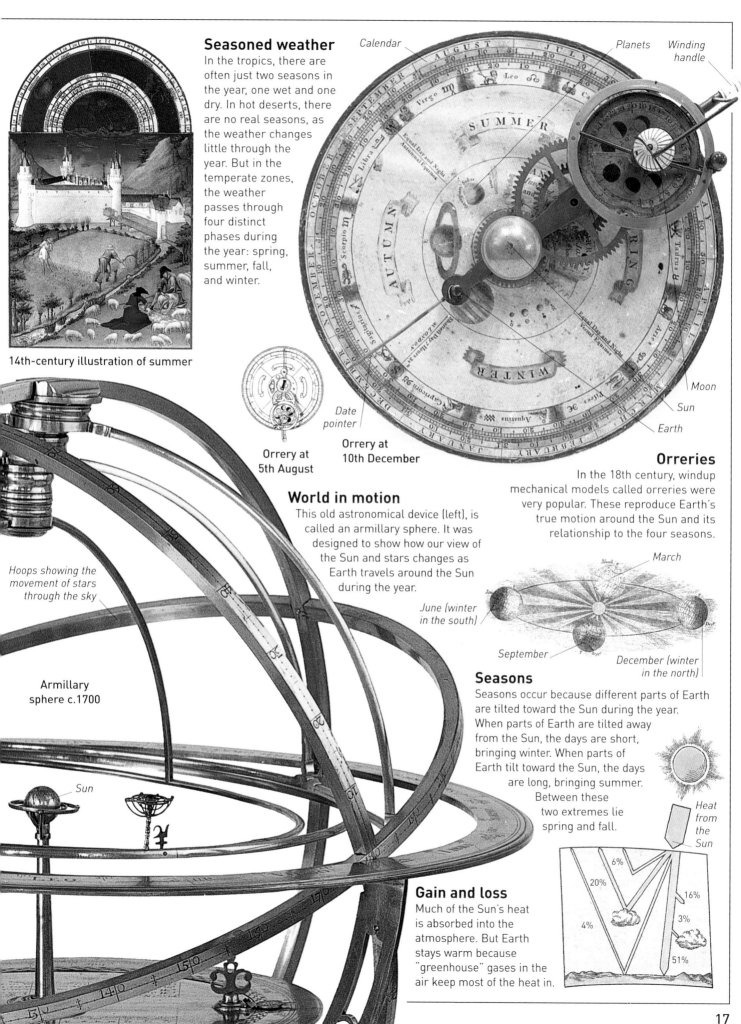

14th-century illustration of summer

Calendar

Planets

Winding handle

Date pointer

Orrery at 10th December

Orrery at 5th August

Moon

Sun

Earth

Orreries

In the 18th century, windup mechanical models called orreries were very popular. These reproduce Earth's true motion around the Sun and its relationship to the four seasons.

World in motion

This old astronomical device (left), is called an armillary sphere. It was designed to show how our view of the Sun and stars changes as Earth travels around the Sun during the year.

March

June (winter in the south)

September

December (winter in the north)

Seasons

Seasons occur because different parts of Earth are tilted toward the Sun during the year. When parts of Earth are tilted away from the Sun, the days are short, bringing winter. When parts of Earth tilt toward the Sun, the days are long, bringing summer. Between these two extremes lie spring and fall.

Hoops showing the movement of stars through the sky

Armillary sphere c.1700

Sun

Heat from the Sun

Gain and loss

Much of the Sun's heat is absorbed into the atmosphere. But Earth stays warm because "greenhouse" gases in the air keep most of the heat in.

6%

20%

16%

4%

3%

51%

17

A sunny day

Over much of the world, sunny weather and clear skies are common, especially in summer. Clouds form only when there is enough moisture in the air and enough movement to carry the moisture high into the atmosphere. Dry, sunny weather is often associated with high pressure, where cold air in the atmosphere sinks slowly, compressing (squashing) the air below and preventing clouds from forming. In summer, high pressure can last for days, bringing long spells of warm, dry weather.

The annual average temperature of Dallol in Ethiopia is 94°F (34.4°C).

Sun god
So important was reliable sunshine in ancient times—not only for heat and light, but also for ripening crops—that many early civilizations worshiped the Sun. The Aztecs of Mexico, in particular, built vast temples to their Sun god, Tonatiuh.

Growing light
Green plants need plenty of sunshine, as all their energy for growth comes directly from the Sun.

Image of the Sun reflected in glass

Burning record
Meteorologists can record hours of sunshine on a device called a Campbell-Stokes sunshine recorder (right). A glass ball focuses the Sun's rays on to a strip of card so that they burn the card. As the Sun moves around during the day, so do the scorch marks on the paper, giving a complete record of the day's sunshine.

Burn marks on card

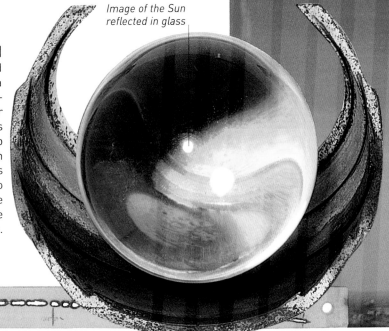

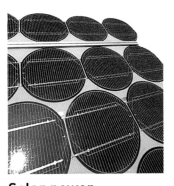

Solar power
Most of our energy comes from the Sun. Light-sensitive crystals in solar cells enable us to convert light energy from the Sun into electricity.

In summer, sunny days tend to be hot, as there is little cloud to block out the Sun's rays. But without clouds to trap the heat rising from the ground, temperatures can often drop rapidly after sunset. Clear, blue skies may look uninteresting at first sight, but there is often plenty going on, especially when the atmosphere is humid or dusty.

Wisps of high cirrus cloud, made entirely of ice. These may be traces of a vanished storm cloud, since ice turns into water vapor more slowly than water. But they could signal the arrival of a warm front.

Remnants of contrails

Trails of water vapor left by jet planes, especially in cold, dry air. Made of ice, these trails of vapor, called contrails, form when the hot gases that shoot out behind a plane hit cool air and rise rapidly. As they rise, they expand and freeze almost immediately.

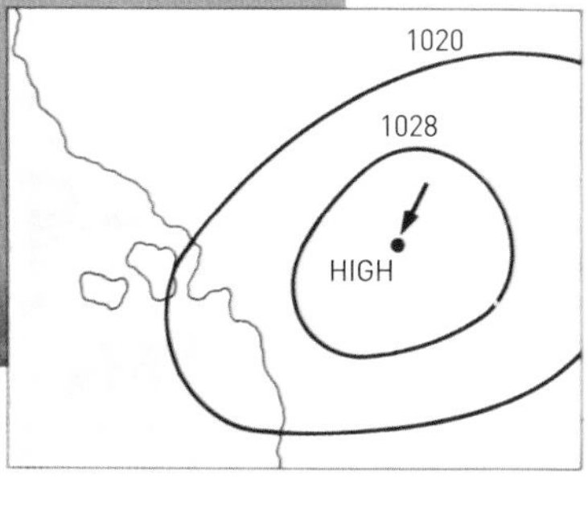

Small, short-lived, fluffy cumulus clouds may be formed here and there by rising warm air currents

Low-level haze, especially over urban areas. Winds may be too light to disperse smoke and dust, and, if the pressure is high, water vapor and pollutants may get trapped in a layer of air just above the ground.

1020

1028

HIGH

Frost and ice

Frosty hands
The fictional "Jack Frost" is said to leave icy finger marks on window panes.

Temperatures are rarely high in winter, and at night, heat in the ground can flow away quickly. On a clear, dry winter night, temperatures near the ground can fall so low that water vapor in the air freezes, forming white crystals called frost. Frosts are rare in the tropics, but are almost continuous toward the poles. In the mid-latitudes, frosts occur more often inland than near the coast, where the sea tends to keep its heat longer.

Icing up
High in the atmosphere, air temperatures are always below freezing, and the wings of airplanes can easily become coated with ice.

Hoar thorns
When water vapor touches a very cold surface, it can freeze instantly, leaving spiked needles of "hoar frost." The frost tends to occur when the temperature is around 32°F (0°C), but the air must be moist to create the ice crystals.

Cold frame
In severe weather, delicate "fern frost" patterns may appear on windows. Drops of moisture called dew form on the cold glass. As they freeze, they turn into ice crystals, forming beautiful patterns.

The low temperatures near the ground that bring frost can also create fog. The moisture condenses in the cold air and hangs there, because there is little wind to disperse it. If the fog coats surfaces with ice, it is called freezing fog.

Thick coating of rime, a white ice formed when an icy wind blows over leaves, branches, and other surfaces. Temperatures usually have to be lower for rime than for hoar frost.

Hoar frost coats freezing cold surfaces, such as soil and metal, with ice crystals.

Frozen arch
Sometimes vast chunks of ice, or icebergs, break off polar glaciers and float out to sea. Icebergs float because water becomes less dense when it freezes, but most of their bulk lies below the water.

Even though there is a mist near the ground, the sky above is clear, allowing heat to escape during the night.

Frost is white because the crystals contain air.

Icy coating

When the conditions are cold enough, moisture from the air freezes, leaving surfaces coated with a thin layer of ice crystals. In spring and fall, frosts can occur when heat rises from the ground on clear nights. In midwinter though, a chill polar wind may be enough to bring frost.

Ice house

Most icicles form when drips of melting snow freeze. This house in Chicago got its remarkable coat of ice when firemen sprayed water on it to put out a fire—on the coldest night in the city's history.

Market on ice

In the early 1800s, frosts could be so hard that even the Thames River in London froze solid. The last "frost fair" held on the ice was in 1814.

Wet air

Even on the sunniest days, the horizon often shimmers in a haze. Some haze is dust and pollution, but most is simply moisture in the air. Like a dry sponge, the air soaks up water that is constantly rising up from Earth's surface. Most of the moisture in the air is in the form of an invisible gas called water vapor. If water vapor cools enough in the air, it turns into droplets of water in a process called condensation. Clouds, mist, and haze are all formed from these tiny droplets.

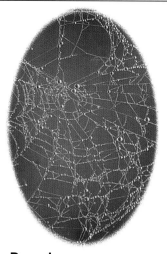

Dew drops
Water vapor condenses as air cools. The cooler the air, the less water vapor it can hold. Once air reaches the limit of moisture it can hold, the water vapor condenses into droplets. This is called the dew point.

Scale shows humidity

Human hair

Hair hygrometer

When the water level in the spout is high, pressure is low and storms can be expected

Closed glass bulb

When working, the level of water in the weather glass would have been much higher

Storm glass
Like mercury in a barometer, water levels can be used to monitor air pressure. Though not as accurate, "weather glasses" like this (above) were cheaper to make than mercury barometers.

Wet hair
Humidity (the moisture content of the air) can be measured using an instrument called a hair hygrometer (above). It contains a piece of human hair that stretches in moist air and shrinks in dry air.

Gruß aus Villach

Weather house
Weather houses like this (left) are actually hair hygrometers. If the air is moist, a hair inside the house stretches and lets the man out. If the air is dry, the hair shrinks, pulling the man in and letting the woman out.

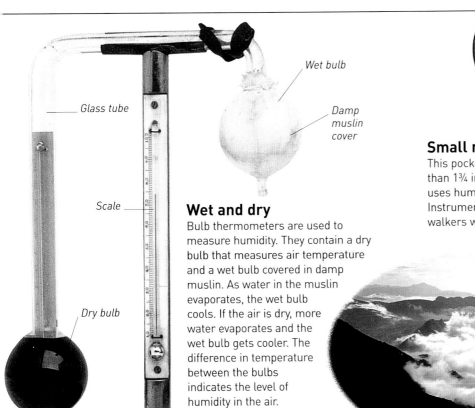

Glass tube

Scale

Dry bulb

Wet bulb

Damp muslin cover

Wet and dry

Bulb thermometers are used to measure humidity. They contain a dry bulb that measures air temperature and a wet bulb covered in damp muslin. As water in the muslin evaporates, the wet bulb cools. If the air is dry, more water evaporates and the wet bulb gets cooler. The difference in temperature between the bulbs indicates the level of humidity in the air.

Antique version of a bulb thermometer

Small measures

This pocket hygrometer—less than 1¾ in (4 cm) in diameter— uses human hair to work the needle. Instruments like this were often used by walkers who wanted to predict a shower.

Mountain mist

In mountain areas, mist will often gather in the valleys in the morning because cold air flows downhill in the night and settles there.

Raindrop just large enough to overcome tension

Small raindrops held on glass by surface tension

Water vision

Even on clear days, there is often a slight haze in the air, making distant hills look soft and pale.

Raindrops

Unless a raindrop is big to start with, a phenomenon known as surface tension will hold it on to a pane of glass until another drop falls in the same place. This breaks the tension, and the drops run down the pane together. In the same way, tiny droplets of water in a cloud will only start to fall as rain when they are large and heavy enough.

Damp trade

Silk-making requires moist air. If the air is not damp enough, the caterpillars will not spin the thread properly.

Large drop gathers others in its path

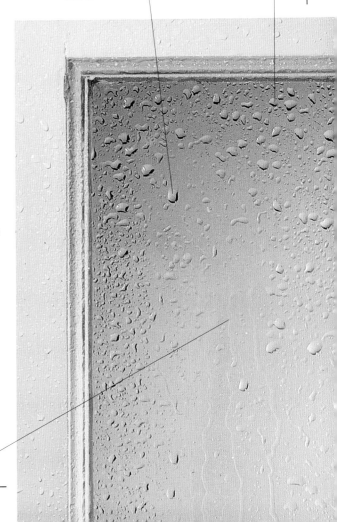

The birth of a cloud

On a clear day, you will often see fleecy, "cotton" clouds constantly changing in shape and size. Every so often, new clouds appear out of the blue, while others shrink and vanish. Short-lived clouds like these are called cumulus, or "heap" clouds. They are formed when the Sun heats a patch of ground, creating a bubble of warm, moist air. The bubble drifts upward, and as it rises, it cools and condenses to form a cloud of tiny water droplets. Bubbles like these rarely last for more than 20 minutes. Often, several new bubbles drift up in the same place. If this happens, the clouds may build up so much that a shower of rain will fall. Occasionally, fleecy cumulus clouds billow high into the atmosphere and turn into huge thunderclouds that will eventually release a terrific downpour.

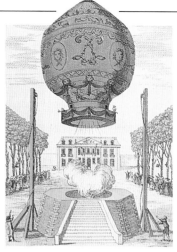

Hot air
As air heats up, it becomes lighter than the cooler air around it and starts to rise. The Montgolfier brothers used this principle when they filled a balloon with hot air to make the first manned flight over Paris, in 1783.

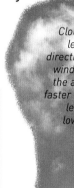

Clouds often lean in the direction of the wind because the air moves faster at higher levels than lower down

Steam clouds
Steam from an engine's funnel forms in much the same way as a cloud. As hot, moist air leaves the funnel, it expands and cools, until it gets so cold that it condenses into water droplets, forming steam.

In the morning, when the thermals are weak, small, individual clouds form, with clear sky between them

3 Building clouds
Clouds disappear only if the surrounding air is dry. They last longer as the day goes by, as the rising air brings in new moisture.

Thermals

Bubbles of warm air, called thermals, form over hot spots on the ground. The warm air drifts up and expands into the cooler air around it. As the air rises, it cools down, until at a certain height—the condensation level—it is so cool that the moisture it contains condenses into water droplets.

Early clouds often disappear, evaporating into the drier surrounding air

2 New bubbles
Sometimes, the clouds formed by bubbles of warm air will drift away in the wind, and others will take their place, creating lines of clouds for many miles.

1 Small beginnings
It takes some time for the Sun to heat the ground, so the first clouds are very small.

Elk's breath

If the air is very cold, moisture in the elk's breath will condense into water droplets, which turn into tiny clouds.

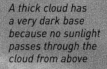

A thick cloud has a very dark base because no sunlight passes through the cloud from above

5 High fliers

The movement of air inside cumulus clouds often becomes organized into "cells," with strong currents of air rising and falling very close to each other. Pilots try to avoid flying through large cumulus clouds because these sudden updrafts and downdrafts of air can lead to a very bumpy ride.

Clouds appear brilliantly white in sunshine because the tiny water droplets reflect light extremely well

4 Up, up, and away

As the day heats up, more thermals drift upward. If one arrives close behind another, a single cloud is created.

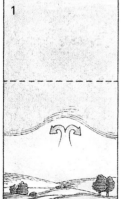
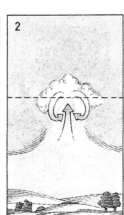

A cloud forms

Clouds form when moist air is lifted high enough into the air to cool and condense (1). The Sun heats a patch of ground, sending up bubbles of rising warm air (2). Fleecy cumulus clouds appear, and disappear when these bubbles no longer form (3).

Artificial clouds

Not all clouds are natural ones. Inside power-plant cooling towers, the large quantities of cool water produce enormous volumes of very moist, slightly warm air, which often condenses immediately above the towers into low, "artificial" cumulus clouds.

A cloudy day

Lingering cloudy skies are usually associated with layered, or stratus, clouds, which build up over a wide area when a warm, moist wind meets colder air. As this warm air rides slowly up over cold air, it steadily condenses as it cools, creating a vast blanket of cloud that can be hundreds of feet thick and stretch for hundreds of miles.

Three kinds of cloud
On some days, several types of cloud can be seen at different heights in the sky. In this picture (right), there are not only stratus and cumulus clouds, but also a third type, called lenticular clouds. These lens-shaped clouds form near mountain ranges, where mountains disturb the airflow and create waves in the wind.

Cloud height
The Victorians calculated the height of clouds using cameras on tripods. Today, meteorologists use laser beams pointed at the base of the cloud. Cloud cover, however, is worked out visually, by estimating roughly what proportion of the sky is covered by the cloud directly overhead.

Small cumulus clouds are unlikely to produce much rain—although there might be light showers late in the day

Stratus cloud

Ups and downs
Glider pilots need rising currents of air, called thermals, to climb upward. Thermals rise up to form cumulus clouds and are common over warm areas of land. However, they will not form over cooler bodies of water, such as lakes, so the gliders sink back down toward the ground. The same thing happens if thick layers of cloud cover the sky and cut off the warmth of the sunlight from the ground.

Thermals rising beneath cumulus clouds

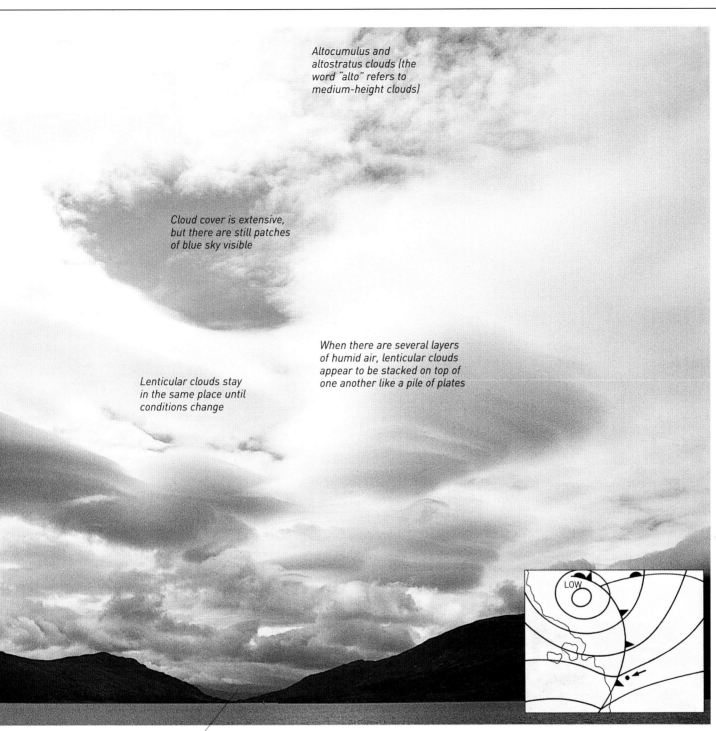

Altocumulus and altostratus clouds (the word "alto" refers to medium-height clouds)

Cloud cover is extensive, but there are still patches of blue sky visible

When there are several layers of humid air, lenticular clouds appear to be stacked on top of one another like a pile of plates

Lenticular clouds stay in the same place until conditions change

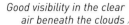
Good visibility in the clear air beneath the clouds

Smooth or lumpy

The Beauty of the Heavens by Charles F. Blunt showed two main groups of clouds: cumulus (left), which are heaped clouds formed by the rise of individual bubbles of air, and cirrostratus (right), where whole layers of air are forced to rise, forming widespread sheets of cloud.

Clouds of all kinds

Luke Howard
Howard (1772–1864) based his system on cloud shapes and heights.

Clouds come in all sorts of shapes, sizes, and colors, from white, wispy "mares' tails" to towering, gray thunderclouds. English pharmacist Luke Howard devised a system of classifying clouds in 1803. He identified 10 distinct categories of cloud, all of which are variations on three basic cloud forms—puffy cumulus clouds, layered stratus clouds, and feathery cirrus clouds. This system is still used by meteorologists today.

Flying saucers
Lens-shaped lenticular clouds form over mountain ranges.

Sheet clouds
Altostratus are high, thin sheets of cloud that can often completely cover the sky, making the Sun look as if it is seen through misty glass.

Temperature here -40°F (-40°C)

Cloud spreads out at the top where the air stops rising at the tropopause (the top of the troposphere). This is sometimes called the "anvil," because it is shaped like a blacksmith's anvil.

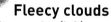

Fleecy clouds
Altocumulus (left) are medium-height, fluffy rolls of cloud with dark, shadowed sides.

A gray blanket
Stratus (left) are vast, dull clouds that hang low over the ground and may give a damp drizzle, but no real rain. Higher up, stratus clouds appear as fog.

Temperature here 32°F (0°C)

Cirrus	12
Cirrostratus	11
Cirrocumulus	10
Altostratus	9
Altocumulus	8
	7
Stratocumulus	6
Cumulus	5
	4
Cumulonimbus	3
	2
Stratus	1
Nimbostratus	Sea level (km)

Cloud heights
Cirrus-type clouds form at the top of the troposphere. Stratocumulus, stratus, nimbostratus, and cumulus are closer to the ground. Cumulonimbus can reach up through the whole troposphere.

Trailing virga

Cumulus clouds sometimes let rain or ice crystals fall into drier, slower-moving layers of air. The streaks that result, known as "virga," evaporate before they reach the ground. From below, they look as if they are vanishing into thin air.

Mares' tails

Cirrus clouds, made entirely from ice crystals, form high in the sky, where strong winds blow the crystals into wispy "mares' tails."

Mainly ice crystals

An icy veil

Cirrostratus occurs when cirrus spreads into a thin, milky sheet. Here the Sun appears very bright and may be surrounded by colored rings.

Cloud moves from left to right

Strong updrafts carry billows of cloud high into the atmosphere

Mixture of ice crystals and water

High, fluffy clouds

Cirrocumulus (right) are made of ice crystals, and often form a pattern known as a "mackerel sky," because the clouds look like the mottled scales of a mackerel.

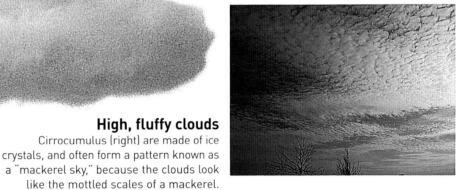

A layer of cumulus

Stratocumulus often form when the tops of cumulus clouds rise and spread out sideways into broad sheets. From above, they appear as a blanket of rolling cloud (right).

Shower clouds

Bigger and darker than cumulus, cumulonimbus (left) often bring thunderstorms and heavy rain.

Violent updrafts and downdrafts in the front wall of cloud create hailstones

Mainly water droplets

Cauliflower clouds

Cumulus clouds often mass together and grow upward, with dense, white heads like cauliflowers. If they keep growing, they may become rain-bearing cumulonimbus.

Air drawn in here

A rainy day

Dark, slate-gray clouds are a sure sign of rain. In the tropics, huge cumulonimbus clouds can tower 9 miles (15 km) into the sky, unleashing sudden torrential downpours. Lighter, thinner nimbostratus clouds provide slow, steady rain that may last for hours, or even days. Low stratus clouds give persistent drizzle that is little more than a mist.

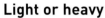

Raining fish
Creatures such as frogs and fish have been known to fall from the sky during storms. They have been lifted up and carried in the air by tornadoes, before being dropped to the ground with the rain.

Light or heavy
Rain is described as light if less than $1/32$ in (0.5 mm) falls in an hour, and heavy if more than 4 mm ($1/4$ in) falls. In the mid-latitudes, heavy rain does not usually last long. Even the worst downpours are rarely heavier than those seen most days in many tropical areas.

Heavy rain fills the air beneath the cloud to the point where further condensation takes place beneath the main base

Cloudburst
A cumulonimbus cloud will start to die when its cold, downward air currents overwhelm its warm upcurrents. At this point, the cloud releases all its water at once in a cloudburst.

The rough texture of the cloud base shows just how violent the vertical air currents are within the clouds

Flooding
Very heavy rain can cause flooding after a long, dry period of drought. The soil becomes so hard that rainwater cannot drain away and runs across the surface instead.

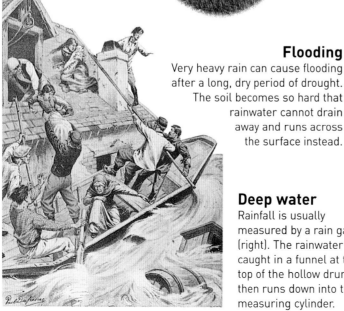

Deep water
Rainfall is usually measured by a rain gauge (right). The rainwater is caught in a funnel at the top of the hollow drum, then runs down into the measuring cylinder.

Water from the funnel collects in the cylinder

Rolls of cloud form as rain sweeps the colder air downward, forcing warm air upward to create another cloud

Rain falling from the base of the cloud

This man with his geese (from a Japanese woodcut) knows that rain is on the way.

Storm waters
Storms at sea can create huge waves that cause flooding in coastal regions.

Deluge
Some of the world's heaviest rain is brought by monsoon winds. In Cherrapunji in India, monsoon rains once brought 16 ft (4.8 m) of rain in 15 days.

Fronts and lows

In the mid-latitudes—the areas between the tropics and the polar regions—much of the year's most unpleasant weather comes from great, spiraling weather systems called depressions, or lows. Depressions produce swirls of cloud that bring cloudy skies, blustery winds, rain, and even snow. A big depression may be hundreds of miles wide, but it usually passes over in less than 24 hours.

Warm front

Wisps of cirrus

Veils of cirrostratus

Wind here light and blowing away from the front

Cold polar air

Wispy warning

When long streaks of wispy cirrus clouds are seen high in the sky, they often signal a change of weather and the onset of a depression. Cirrus clouds form right at the top of a warm front (see below), and are made entirely of ice.

A warm front

When a mass of warm, tropical air meets cold polar air, a boundary called a front develops between them. A warm front often signals the arrival of a depression. Here, the warm, moist tropical air slides up over a wedge of cold, polar air, producing clouds. As the front moves forward, cirrus clouds form at the edge, followed by a veil of cirrostratus clouds. Within a few hours, the clouds thicken at the base of the front, first with altostratus, and then with great, gray nimbostratus. The sky grows dark, and rain—or even snow—starts to fall. The rain lasts for several hours before clearing up to give a short break before the cold front arrives.

Wind here blowing strongly almost parallel to the front

Each to its own

Each part of the world has its own type of air mass, bringing its own kind of weather. Warm, wet, tropical ocean air brings warm, humid weather, while cold, wet, polar ocean air can bring snow.

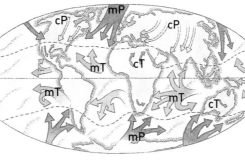

Tropical continental (cT)
Polar continental (cP)
Tropical maritime (mT)
Polar maritime (mP)

Air masses

There is a close link between the direction of the wind and the weather. Wind and weather are linked by air masses—vast chunks of the atmosphere that are either wet or dry, or cold or warm throughout. Dry, cold air masses form over continents near the poles, while warm, moist ones form over tropical oceans. To a large extent, the weather depends on which air mass is overhead at the time. Far inland, a single air mass can stay in place for a long period of time, bringing stable weather. In coastal areas, a shift in wind direction can bring a different air mass and a change in the weather. The most changeable, stormy weather tends to occur along a front—the point at which two air masses meet.

Veiled warning

When the Sun is faintly visible through a thin veil of altostratus, it is time to begin seeking shelter, since rain is not far away.

First rain

As the front approaches, the sky darkens and the first drops of rain may fall—even before the thick nimbostratus clouds arrive.

Cold air descending at the front

Thickening altostratus

Warm tropical air riding up over the cold air

Dark, rain-bearing nimbostratus

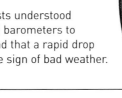

Barometer dial indicating changeable, possibly stormy weather

Rain falls in the cold section beneath the front

Falling dial

Long before meteorologists understood depressions, sailors used barometers to predict storms. They found that a rapid drop in air pressure was a sure sign of bad weather.

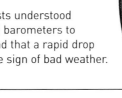

Continued on next page

A cold front

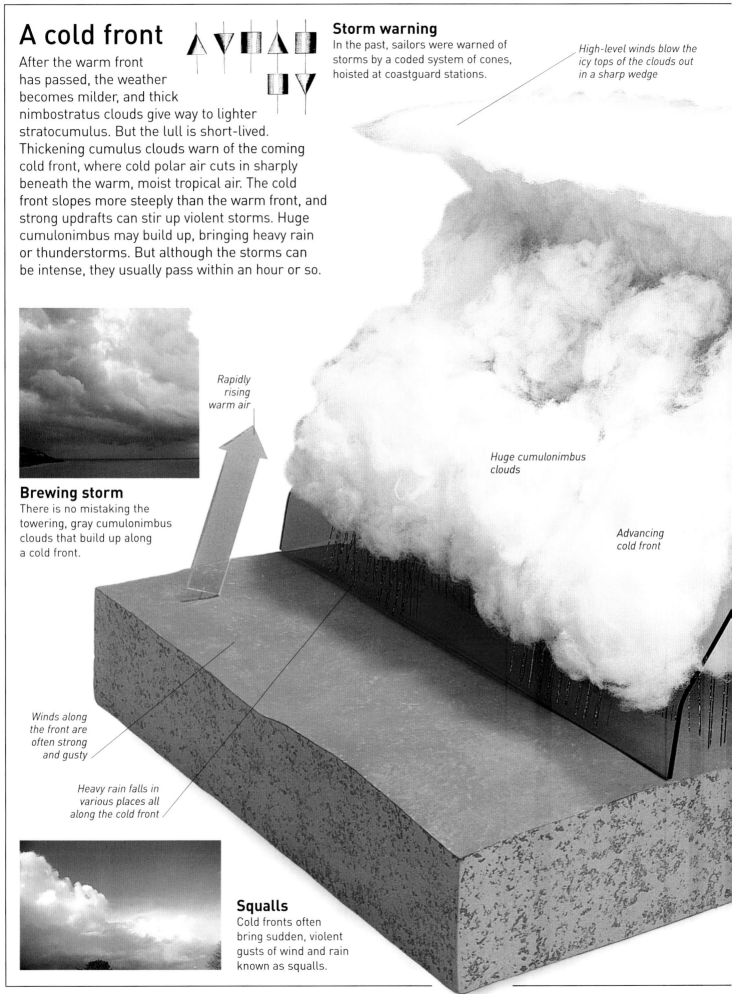

After the warm front has passed, the weather becomes milder, and thick nimbostratus clouds give way to lighter stratocumulus. But the lull is short-lived. Thickening cumulus clouds warn of the coming cold front, where cold polar air cuts in sharply beneath the warm, moist tropical air. The cold front slopes more steeply than the warm front, and strong updrafts can stir up violent storms. Huge cumulonimbus may build up, bringing heavy rain or thunderstorms. But although the storms can be intense, they usually pass within an hour or so.

Storm warning
In the past, sailors were warned of storms by a coded system of cones, hoisted at coastguard stations.

High-level winds blow the icy tops of the clouds out in a sharp wedge

Rapidly rising warm air

Huge cumulonimbus clouds

Advancing cold front

Brewing storm
There is no mistaking the towering, gray cumulonimbus clouds that build up along a cold front.

Winds along the front are often strong and gusty

Heavy rain falls in various places all along the cold front

Squalls
Cold fronts often bring sudden, violent gusts of wind and rain known as squalls.

As the front moves away to the east, the skies clear, leaving a few cumulus clouds toward the setting Sun. High above, strong winds in the upper atmosphere create dramatic streaks of icy clouds across the sky.

Strong updrafts of air carry moisture so high that it turns to ice

The diagrams below show how a depression forms in the northern hemisphere; for the south, hold a mirror above each picture.

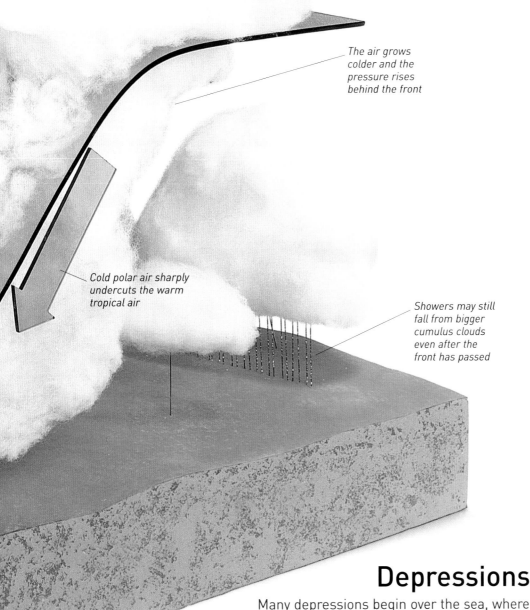

The air grows colder and the pressure rises behind the front

Cold polar air sharply undercuts the warm tropical air

Showers may still fall from bigger cumulus clouds even after the front has passed

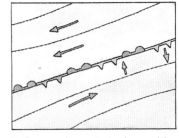

1. Depressions start when cold polar air and warm tropical air meet at the polar front.

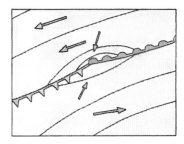

2. The two air masses rotate around an area of low pressure caused by rising warm air.

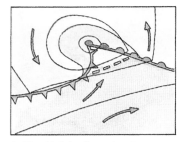

3. The kink in the polar front develops two arms—the warm front and the cold front.

Depressions

Many depressions begin over the sea, where warm, moist, tropical air collides with cold, dry, polar air along an imaginary line called the "polar front." A depression starts when the warm tropical air bulges into the polar air. As the warm air rises, it creates an area of low pressure. The cold air rushes in to replace the rising warm air, causing the winds to spiral. As the depression deepens, the polar front develops a definite kink. Along one edge, the warm air rises slowly over the cold air in a gradual slope (the warm front). Along the other, the cold air thrusts sharply under the warm air from behind (the cold front).

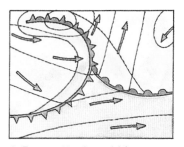

4. Eventually, the cold front catches up with the warm front, lifting it off the ground.

Thunder and lightning

When a black, towering cumulonimbus cloud unleashes a deluge of thunder, lightning, wind, and rain, the effect can be awe-inspiring. Big thunderclouds can tower 10 miles (16 km) or more in the air and create enough energy to light a small town for a year. Cumulonimbus clouds are formed by strong, turbulent updrafts of hot, moist air. They are most common in the tropics, where massive storms often break in the afternoon, after the morning Sun has stirred up the air.

Thunderstruck
The heavy hammer carried by Thor, the Norse god of thunder, represented the "thunderbolt" that was thought to fall from the clouds.

It's electric
In 1752, US inventor Benjamin Franklin carried out experiments with kites to prove that lightning was electricity.

Lightning
Thunderclouds are heaving masses of air, water, and ice. Inside, violent air currents cause ice crystals to smash into each other, causing static electricity. Ice crystals at the base of the cloud become negatively charged, while the ground and the top of the cloud are positively charged. The difference in electrical charges becomes so great that electricity starts leaping between different parts of the cloud (sheet lightning) or between the cloud and the ground (fork lightning).

Storm god
To ward off violent storms, priests in Nigeria prayed to the storm god, Sango.

Strike!
Lightning tends to strike tall objects like trees, which is why it is dangerous to shelter under one in a storm.

Having a ball
People have reported a strange phenomenon called ball lightning. In 1773, there were reports of a glowing ball in a fireplace that burst with a loud bang. These rare sightings have never been explained.

You can tell how far away a storm is by counting the number of seconds between seeing the lightning and hearing the thunder. This is because light travels faster than sound. A gap of two seconds means the storm is about half a mile away.

Hail and hearty

A section of one of the largest hailstones ever found, which weighed 1¾ lb (768 g), fell in Coffeyville, Kansas, in 1970. Special illumination shows that it is made of alternate layers of clear and opaque ice.

Cumulonimbus clouds still growing upward

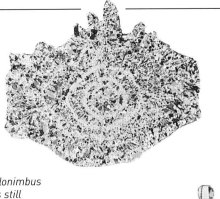

Storm shooting

Hail can devastate crops. In 1900, many people shot debris into the clouds to stop hail from forming. These anti-hail guns injured people on the ground, but the hail was just as heavy.

As a lightning bolt flashes through the air, the air around becomes five times as hot as the surface of the Sun. The air expands at supersonic speed, making the mighty crash called thunder.

Lightning always takes the easiest path from cloud to ground

Lightning bolts begin when a small "leader stroke" zigzags to the ground

A split second after the leader stroke, a massive surge of lightning—the "return stroke"—shoots up the path it created

Monsoon

For six months of the year, most of India is parched and dry. But every May, the monsoon comes. A moist wind blows in from the Indian Ocean and the skies grow dark with clouds. For six months, torrential rain sweeps north over the country until the wind dies down and the rains slacken. By December, the land is dry once more. Similar rainy seasons occur in many other places in the tropics, such as northeast Australia and East Africa.

The monsoon can lash tropical coasts with intense rain, wind, thunder, and lightning.

The monsoon brings some of the world's most torrential rains

Band of rain moving rapidly across open grassland

Dragon's breath
The monsoon rains are vital for crops in most of Asia. In China they were symbolized by the dragon, who brought the precious gift of water.

Wind disk for tracking the path of the typhoon

Heavy needle lines up with the normal path of storms in the region

Thin needle indicates a safe course away from the storm

After the deluge
Monsoon rains can cause severe flooding. In India and Bangladesh, the low-lying delta of the Ganges River is particularly prone to floods.

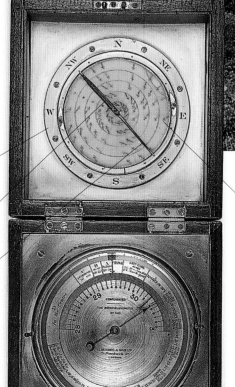

Typhoon barometer

Arrows on the disk show wind direction over the ship

Typhoon tracker
Ships sailing in monsoon regions used to carry an instrument called a "baryocyclometer" (left) to help them track the path of a storm. Now most rely on broadcast warnings.

High cumulonimbus clouds

Large cumulonimbus clouds pile up against high ground as the monsoon blows inland

Mountains force the monsoon upward causing even more rain: Cherrapunji in the Assam mountains is one of the wettest places in the world

Some areas may stay dry and parched even while neighboring areas are being drenched

The monsoon comes

The monsoon begins when the summer Sun heats up tropical continents faster than the oceans around. Warm air rising over the land draws in cool, moist air from the sea, while the rain-bearing winds move slowly farther inland. Sometimes the monsoon winds fail to bring any rain to the hot, dry lands, causing crops to fail.

Monsoon region

Monsoons affect large areas of the tropics, from the Caribbean to northeast Australia.

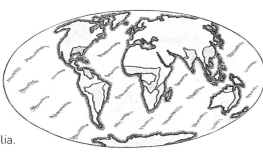

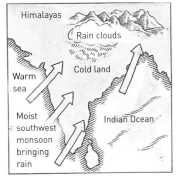

Southwest monsoon

The hot, dry lands of Asia draw warm, moist air from the Indian Ocean in early summer.

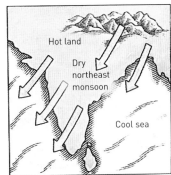

Northeast monsoon

The cold, dry winter air spreads out from central Asia, bringing chilly, dusty conditions.

A snowy day

Snow forms when tiny ice crystals in clouds stick together to form snowflakes. Outside the tropics, most rain starts off as snow, but it usually melts before it reaches the ground. The heaviest snowfalls occur when the air temperature is hovering around freezing. If the weather is too cold, the air cannot hold enough moisture to produce rain or snow. In fact, more snow falls in a year in southern Canada and the northern US than at the North Pole.

Snow rescue
Freshly fallen snow contains so much air that people can survive beneath it for a long time.

Under very cold conditions snow remains loose and powdery, and it is often whipped up by the wind

Fresh snow can contain as much as 90–95 percent air and protects the ground from much colder temperatures above the surface

Rivers of ice and air
Snow builds up on high ground where temperatures are low. It turns into ice, which slowly flows down valleys as glaciers. Cold, heavy air above the ice caps follows the same paths, bringing icy winds to the lowlands beneath.

A cold blanket
Once snow has covered the ground, it is often slow to melt because it reflects away the sunlight. If the surface melts and then refreezes, the snow cover will last even longer.

Snowflakes
Snowflakes occur in a variety of shapes, and no two are identical. All natural snowflakes are made of ice crystals and have six sides.

The snowflake man
W. A. Bentley was an American farmer who spent more than 40 years photographing snowflakes through a microscope.

"Tablecloth" of stratus cloud caused by gentle airflow over the mountains

On average, 12 in (30.5 cm) of snow is equal to 1 in (2.5 cm) of rain

Melting and refreezing causes a harder surface crust

Swirling winds always cause more snow to fall in one place than in another, leading to drifts, which tend to grow larger and larger

Air from Arctic

LOW

Windy— indicated by isobar lines close together

Avalanche

Avalanches happen when fresh, loose snow builds up on a harder, icy layer. The slightest disturbance can start a slide, which crashes downhill, burying everything in its path.

Blizzard

In blizzard conditions, snowfall is accompanied by strong winds. The wind piles up huge drifts of snow against any obstacles; the snow may completely cover cars and trains, trapping the passengers inside.

Wind

Wind is the movement of air around Earth. Sometimes it moves slowly, giving a gentle breeze. At other times it moves rapidly, creating gales or hurricanes. Gentle or fierce, wind always starts in the same way. As the Sun moves through the sky, it heats up some parts of the sea and land more than others. The warm air above these hot spots becomes lighter than the surrounding air and begins to rise. Elsewhere, cool air sinks because it is heavier. Winds blow wherever there are differences in the temperature of the air.

Wind tower
In the 1st century BCE, the Greek astronomer Andronicus built an eight-sided Tower of Winds (above). Each face was carved with one of the eight wind spirits, one for each direction the wind blew.

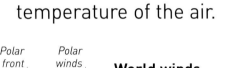

High up, strong jet streams circle the globe
Polar front
Polar winds
Warm tropical air flowing to poles
Westerlies
Easterlies

World winds
The world's winds are part of a global system that moves air between the equator and the poles. At the poles, cold air sinks and moves toward the equator. At the equator, warm air rises and moves toward the poles. Because Earth is spinning, winds do not travel in straight lines. They bend to the right north of the equator and to the left in the south. This bending of the winds is called the Coriolis Effect. Wind direction is always given as the direction from which the wind is blowing, so winds from the west are known as westerlies and those from the east are easterlies.

Head points into the wind, indicating the direction the wind is blowing from

Vane warning
Weather vanes swing around to show where the wind is blowing from. In Christian countries, vanes are often in the form of weather roosters (above). Weather roosters first adorned church roofs in the 9th century CE, as a reminder of the rooster that crowed when St. Peter denied Christ three times.

Catching the wind
Long, thin flags like this pennant (far left) were often flown on ships to show which way the wind was blowing. In the Middle Ages, similar colorful pennants would flutter over battlefields. Archers would use them to figure out the wind direction when aiming their bows.

Cross indicating north, east, south, and west

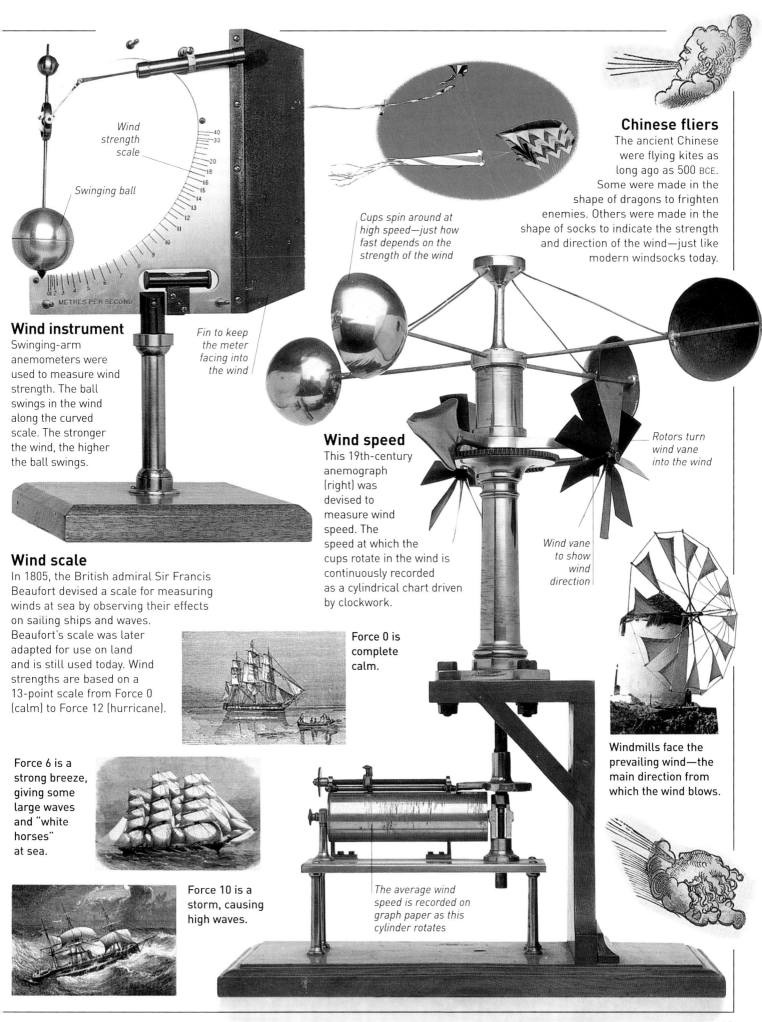

Wind instrument

Swinging-arm anemometers were used to measure wind strength. The ball swings in the wind along the curved scale. The stronger the wind, the higher the ball swings.

Wind strength scale

Swinging ball

METRES PER SECOND

Fin to keep the meter facing into the wind

Wind scale

In 1805, the British admiral Sir Francis Beaufort devised a scale for measuring winds at sea by observing their effects on sailing ships and waves. Beaufort's scale was later adapted for use on land and is still used today. Wind strengths are based on a 13-point scale from Force 0 (calm) to Force 12 (hurricane).

Cups spin around at high speed—just how fast depends on the strength of the wind

Chinese fliers

The ancient Chinese were flying kites as long ago as 500 BCE. Some were made in the shape of dragons to frighten enemies. Others were made in the shape of socks to indicate the strength and direction of the wind—just like modern windsocks today.

Wind speed

This 19th-century anemograph (right) was devised to measure wind speed. The speed at which the cups rotate in the wind is continuously recorded as a cylindrical chart driven by clockwork.

Rotors turn wind vane into the wind

Wind vane to show wind direction

Force 0 is complete calm.

Force 6 is a strong breeze, giving some large waves and "white horses" at sea.

Force 10 is a storm, causing high waves.

The average wind speed is recorded on graph paper as this cylinder rotates

Windmills face the prevailing wind—the main direction from which the wind blows.

Tropical storms

Also known as typhoons and tropical cyclones, hurricanes are the most violent and destructive storms on Earth. Raging winds can gust up to 220 mph (360 kph) and vast areas are swamped by torrential rain. Hurricanes begin as small storms over warm, tropical oceans. If the sea temperature is above 80°F (27°C), several storms may cluster and swirl together, fed by strong winds in the atmosphere. Soon they drift westward across the ocean, drawing in warm, moist air and spinning in ever-tighter circles. At first the eye (center) of the storm may be more than 200 miles (300 km) across. As it moves west, it gains energy from the warm air it draws in. By the time it reaches the far side of the ocean, the eye has shrunk to 30 miles (50 km) across, and winds howl around it at hurricane force.

Hurricane winds can damage or flatten buildings

Anatomy of a hurricane
The air in the eye of the hurricane is calm. As the eye passes directly overhead, the winds may drop, and a circle of clear sky may be visible for a while. The rain and winds are at their worst in the eye wall, a circular wall of cloud surrounding the eye. Here, winds gust at speeds of at least 75 mph (120 kph), although spiraling bands of rain and wind can occur up to 240 miles (400 km) away.

Mixed blessing
Much of the vegetation on tropical islands depends on the torrential rain brought by hurricanes. But the raging winds can also destroy crops.

The strongest winds, with gusts up to 220 mph (360 kph), are found beneath the eye wall, immediately outside the eye

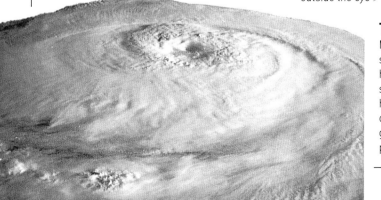

Tracking
Meteorologists use satellite images to track hurricanes. Special aircraft are sent to obtain measurements that help predict the violence and likely path of the storm. Since 1954, names have been given to all tropical storms and cyclones to prevent confusion when issuing forecasts.

   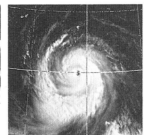 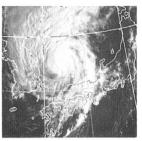

(1) Day 1: thunderstorms develop over the sea.

(2) Day 2: storms group to form a swirl of cloud.

(3) Day 4: winds grow and a distinct center forms.

(4) Day 7: eye forms, typhoon is at its most dangerous.

(5) Day 11: eye moves over land, typhoon starts to die.

Pacific hurricane

The satellite images above show a typhoon forming over the Pacific Ocean. It begins when warm air rises from the ocean forming huge cumulonimbus clouds and bands of thunderstorms (1). Gradually, a swirl of clouds develops (2). The winds become stronger and rotate around a single center (3). An eye develops, just inside the ring of the most destructive and violent winds (4). When the storm passes over land, it loses its source of energy, and the winds drop rapidly (5).

Ice forms at the very top of the clouds

A vast shield of clouds, caused by air spreading out from the top of the storm

Warm, moist air spirals up around the eye inside the hurricane

Hurricanes are enormous. Some may be as much as 480 miles (800 km) across

Heat from the warm sea provides the energy needed to drive the storm

Eye wall

Spiral rain bands

Calm eye of hurricane, where winds may be no more than 15 mph (25 kph)

Air descends in the eye, leaving it clear of cloud

Winds well above 100 mph (160 kph) occur over a large area beneath the storm

Albany hurricane

Hurricanes were far more dangerous when their approach was unexpected. In 1940, the fringes of a hurricane struck Albany, Georgia, without adequate warning, destroying numerous buildings and killing several people.

Whirling winds

Tornadoes, also known as twisters and whirlwinds, are whirling spirals of wind that leave a trail of destruction wherever they strike. The deadly funnel of spinning air roars past in just a few minutes, sucking people, cars, and buildings high into the air, before smashing them to the ground. Tornadoes form inside giant storm clouds called supercells, and they may strike wherever there are thunderstorms.

Mild spin
Tornadoes are especially violent in the American Midwest, but they can strike wherever thunderstorms occur, as shown in this engraving of a whirlwind in England.

Supercell cloud

Funnel touching down in a whirling spray of dust and debris

1 Swirling column
Tornadoes form within vast thunderclouds, where a column of rising warm air is set spinning by high winds at the top of the cloud. The air spins so fast that it forms a "funnel" descending from the cloud's base.

Crop circles
Whirling winds may be the cause of the mysterious circles of flattened crops that appear at random in summer.

2 Whirling devil
As the funnel touches the ground, the tremendous updraft in its center swirls dust, debris, cars, and people high into the sky. Chunks of wood and other objects become deadly missiles as they are hurled through the air by the ferocious winds. A tornado reduces houses in its path to matchwood and rubble, yet can leave those just a few yards outside its path completely untouched. Sometimes a tornado will whirl things high into the air, then set them gently down, unharmed, hundreds of yards away.

Waterspout

When a tornado occurs over the sea, it is called a waterspout. These often last longer than tornadoes, but tend to be gentler, with wind speeds of less than 50 mph (80 kph).

Dusty menace

Unlike tornadoes and waterspouts, which spin down from clouds, "dust devils" are formed in the desert by columns of hot air whirling up from the ground. Though weaker than tornadoes, they can still cause damage.

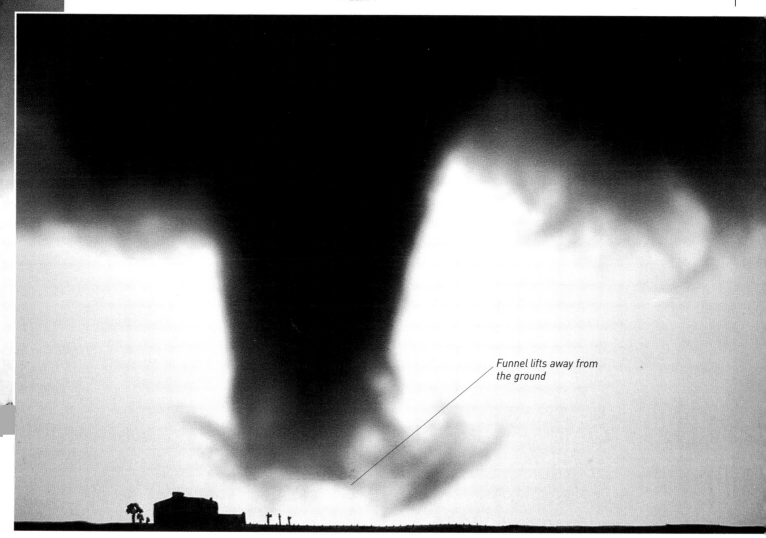

Flying roofs

The strong winds of tornadoes can lift off the roofs of houses. When the roof is whisked away, the rest of the house disintegrates.

Funnel lifts away from the ground

3 Spinning funnels

For a moment, the funnel lifts away from the ground and the houses beneath are safe. But any second it may touch down again. This is a large tornado, and within it there is not just one spinning funnel, but several, each revolving around the main one.

Fog

Lighthouse
In very dense fog, sailors may not be able to see the warning lights of lighthouses and have to rely on foghorns and sirens.

When the wind is light, skies are clear, and the air is damp, moisture in the air can turn into water droplets near the ground, forming mist or fog. The fog clears when the Sun comes up and begins to warm the air. Radiation fog is the most common type of fog. It forms when heat from the ground radiates (escapes) into space. The air above the ground cools and condenses into droplets, forming fog that spreads slowly upward. Fog also forms by advection, where a warm, moist wind blows over a cool surface.

Over the sea, temperature does not always fall far enough to form fog

California fog
In San Francisco, the Golden Gate Bridge (right) is often engulfed in thick advection fog that rolls in from the Pacific. It forms when warm, moist air from the south blows over cool ocean currents flowing from the Arctic. As it moves inland, the fog quickly evaporates as it moves over the warm surface of the land.

Smog
Urban areas are prone to thick fog because they are often situated in low-lying areas close to water. When fog combines with smoke, it forms heavy, polluted air called smog. In some cities, cyclists wear masks to protect them from smog caused by cars and factories.

Pea-souper
Heavy industry and millions of coal fires in homes once made London so dirty that the city became famous for its thick fogs, called "pea-soupers," when visibility would drop to 50 ft (15 m) or less. Since the 1950s, cleaner air has reduced the number of fogs dramatically, and pea-soupers are now a thing of the past.

*Light winds
bring in new air
to sustain mist*

*Fog is actually tiny
droplets of water
condensed from the air*

*Fog spreads slowly
upward from the
surface of the water*

Two fogs

Some coastal fog is a mixture of both radiation and advection fog. On a warm day, a sea breeze may bring cool, moist air inland. At night, most of this drifts back to sea. Some sea air may linger and cool until it condenses to form fog.

Upside down

Fog forms just above the ground, or water, and spreads upward, but only so far. The air actually gets warmer around 1,650 ft (500 m) above the ground. This is called a temperature inversion, and fog does not rise above this point. Inversions like this are common in places like San Diego (right).

A day of weather

The weather can change dramatically during the course of a single day. In many tropical regions, clear, sunny mornings are followed by a massive buildup of thunderclouds as the Sun stirs up strong updrafts of air. Usually this is followed by a brief downpour in the afternoon and a clear dusk. In the mid-latitudes, changes in the weather are often caused by a depression, which can turn warm sunshine into icy rain in just a few hours.

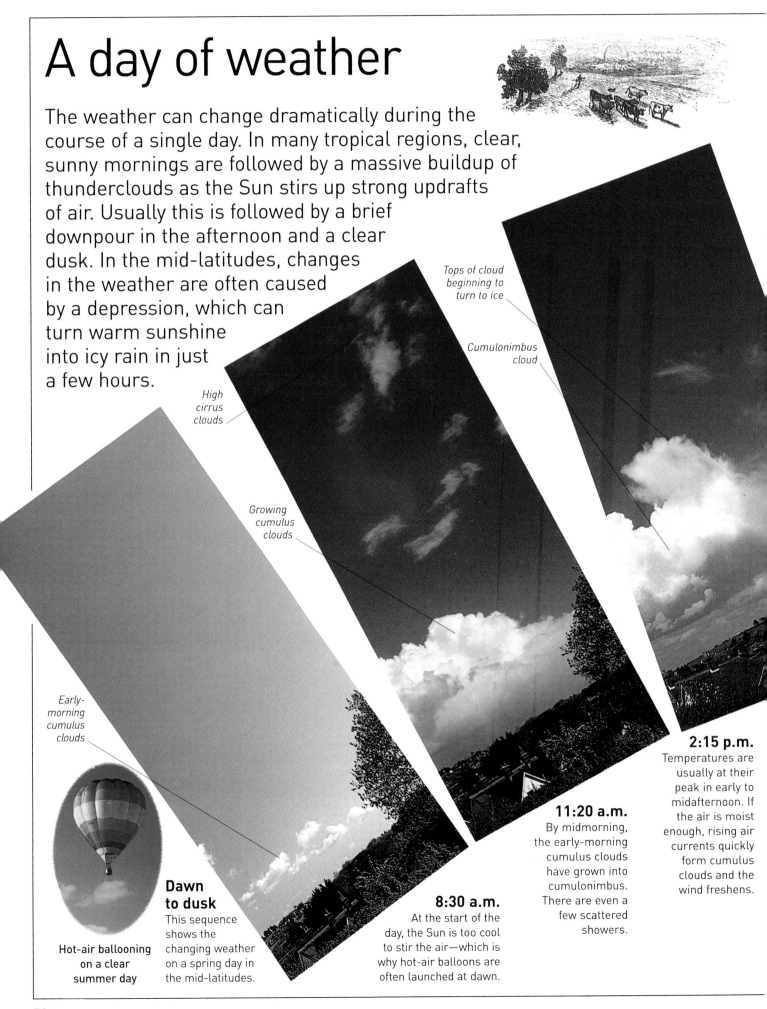

Tops of cloud beginning to turn to ice

Cumulonimbus cloud

High cirrus clouds

Growing cumulus clouds

Early-morning cumulus clouds

2:15 p.m.
Temperatures are usually at their peak in early to midafternoon. If the air is moist enough, rising air currents quickly form cumulus clouds and the wind freshens.

11:20 a.m.
By midmorning, the early-morning cumulus clouds have grown into cumulonimbus. There are even a few scattered showers.

8:30 a.m.
At the start of the day, the Sun is too cool to stir the air—which is why hot-air balloons are often launched at dawn.

Dawn to dusk
This sequence shows the changing weather on a spring day in the mid-latitudes.

Hot-air ballooning on a clear summer day

Icy head of cloud spread out by high level winds

Sky thick with cloud

Sky starting to lighten behind cloud

Rain heavy in places

Rain

3:00 p.m.
By midafternoon, clouds can build up so much that thunderstorms occur. Here, clusters of clouds have joined together—storms, heavy rain, and hail are nearby.

3:45 p.m.
The sky is still darkened by a huge, gray cumulonimbus cloud, its top hidden by the widespread lower clouds around the edge of the storm. Gusts of wind warn of the downdrafts and torrential rain to come.

5:15 p.m.
The heavy clouds start to move away, although rain is still falling. Sunlight strikes through the cloud illuminating the raindrops and creating a rainbow.

Rainbow

Castles in the air
If a layer of warm air forms over a cold sea, distorted images of distant objects can sometimes be seen in the water. They are created when the warm air bends light rays from images of objects that are normally invisible beyond the horizon.

7:00 p.m.
By sunset, the wind has dropped and the band of showers has moved away, leaving a few scattered cumulus clouds. In contrast to the clear sky of the morning, middle-level clouds show that an area of low pressure is approaching from the west bringing unsettled weather.

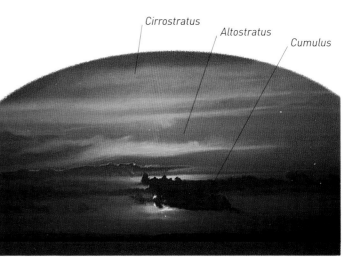

Cirrostratus

Altostratus

Cumulus

Mountains

At the top of Mount Everest, winds howl at up to 200 mph (320 kph), and the temperature often drops as low as −94°F (−70°C). Even on lower mountains, winds tend to be much stronger than down on the plains. Above a certain height—known as the snowline—many mountains are permanently coated in snow and ice. Because mountains reach so far into the atmosphere, they have an effect on wind and cloud patterns, forcing air to move up or down as it passes over their peaks.

Barometer used for measuring air pressure

At the top
Many weather stations are built on mountaintops. At Mt. Washington, New Hampshire, temperatures are below −22°F (−30°C), winds gust at 100 mph (160 kph), and dense fog is common.

Low pressure
In 1648, French scientist Blaise Pascal proved that the atmosphere had its own weight, or pressure. He measured the air pressure at the top and bottom of a mountain and found that the pressure was lower at the top because there was less air weighing down on it from above.

Clouds and snow
In many mountain ranges, the highest peaks may reach above the clouds, basking in bright sunshine. However, the peaks are usually icy cold, since any heat from the Sun is reflected straight back into the atmosphere by the snow. Near the equator, only the very highest peaks are permanently covered in snow, since it is too cold here for rain. Toward the poles, however, the snowline is much lower.

Peaks stand clear of the clouds

Wisps of icy cloud

Permanent snow cover

At night, cold air may drain into the valleys, making them very cold

Wet peaks
The tops of mountains tend to be wet and misty—especially if they reach into a moist air stream. Pacific island mountains, like these in Tahiti (left), are among the dampest places in the world. Mount Wai-ʻale-ʻale in Hawaii is permanently surrounded by wet cloud and receives more than 457 in (11,600 mm) of rain each year.

North-facing slopes are always in deep shadow, and bitterly cold—so cold that ice breaks up the rocks making them steep and craggy

Air pushed up the mountain slopes often fills valleys with clouds

Alpines
Tiny flowers, called alpines, have managed to adapt to the cold, sunny weather of mountains such as the Alps in Europe.

High winds
Mountain tops are nearly always windier than open, low country. This is partly because wind strength increases with height, and partly because winds rush over, rather than around, mountain peaks.

Air warms and dries as it descends over the leeward side

Leeward side

Rising air cools and condenses into clouds

Rain at the summit

Moist air is forced upward by mountain range

Windward side

Air lift
When warm, moist air moves toward a mountain range, it is forced upward. As it rises, it cools and condenses to form heavy rain-bearing clouds that make the slope on the windward side very wet. As the air passes over the mountains, it warms and loses its moisture, leaving the leeward (downwind) side of the mountain much drier. This is known as the rain shadow effect.

On the plains

Far from the sea, the world's vast, flat plains tend to have hot summers and dry, cold winters. Rain falls mostly in the summer when the strong Sun stirs up heavy showers and thunderstorms. In winter, rainfall is rare, although fall snowstorms may deposit a covering that lasts until spring. In the shadow of mountain ranges, many plains are so dry that only scrub, or grass, can grow.

Winter hunters

Millions of buffalo once roamed the North American grasslands, providing food for Native American tribes. The hunters wore snowshoes to keep their feet from sinking into the snow.

Hot blast

Plains on the leeward side of mountains are often subject to hot winds coming down from the mountains. Winds such as the North American Chinook and the Arabian Simoom, shown in this engraving (left), are typical.

Wave clouds

Mountain ranges often disturb winds blowing across them, forming waves of cloud that hover for hours in the upper atmosphere.

Skies are often clear, giving hot summers and cold winters

Extreme weather

Clear, dry skies over the plains can lead to extreme variations in temperature. Winters are bitter, with temperatures well below freezing. In summer, the hot temperatures of the day drop sharply once the Sun goes down.

Parched lands

Most of the world's deserts are plains, such as the Nevada desert (left). Air over the desert warms as it descends, creating dry conditions. It then moves outward, preventing moist air from entering the plain.

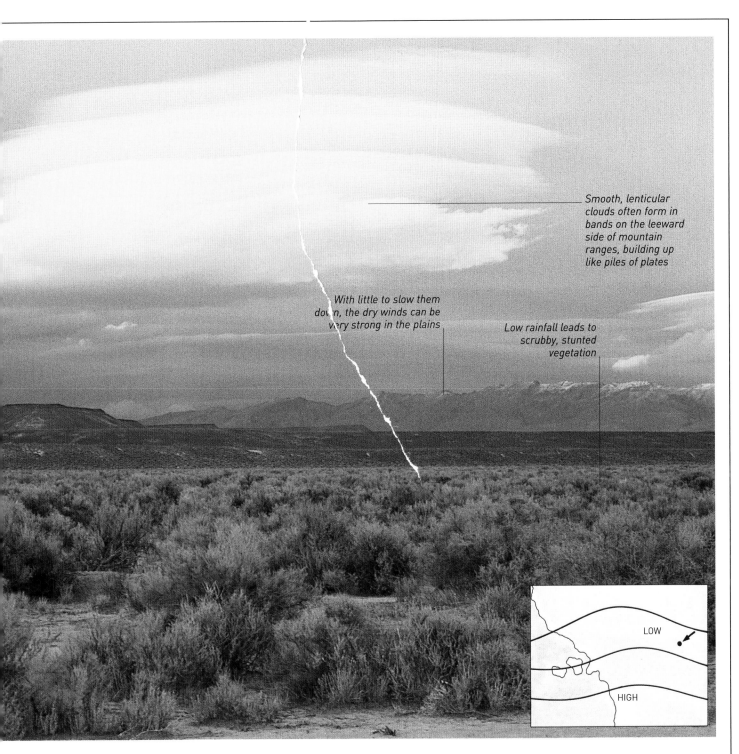

Smooth, lenticular clouds often form in bands on the leeward side of mountain ranges, building up like piles of plates

With little to slow them down, the dry winds can be very strong in the plains

Low rainfall leads to scrubby, stunted vegetation

LOW

HIGH

Sizzling summers
Summer on the plains can be extremely hot. On July 10, 1913, temperatures in Death Valley, California (above), reached 134°F (56.7°C).

Dust Bowl
In the 1930s, the American Midwest suffered a serious drought. Strong winds blew clouds of thick, choking dust from the ground, forcing many families to leave their farms.

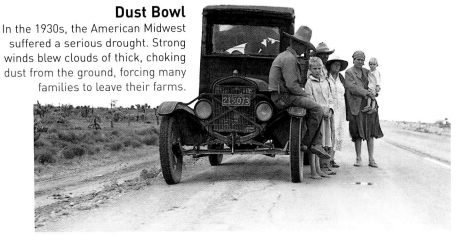

Coastal areas

The presence of so much water gives weather by the sea its own particular characteristics. Coastal areas tend to be wetter and cloudier than inland areas. Cumulus clouds, for instance, usually form inland only during the day, but on coasts facing the wind they drift overhead at night as well. Sea fogs, known as advection fogs, can linger for days and are caused by warm air blowing over cool water. The weather in coastal areas is generally less extreme than farther inland. Because the sea loses heat slowly, nights tend to be warmer on the coast, with milder winters and slightly cooler summers. Frosts are rare on sea coasts in the mid-latitudes.

Frequent, salt-laden winds blowing from the sea dry the exposed sides of trees and shrubs, killing leaves and buds so the plants look as though they are leaning away from the wind

Blown away
Seaside resorts can often be very windy, as illustrated in this 20th-century postcard. This is partly because there are no obstacles across the open sea to stop the winds from blowing hard, and partly because temperature differences between land and sea often create stiff breezes.

Clear coast
This picture (top) shows the coast of Oregon in the northwestern US, but it is typical of west coasts everywhere in the mid-latitudes. Deep depressions are common at this latitude and here, a cold front has just passed over and is moving inland. Cloud lingers in the upper air, and cumulus clouds are still forming, signaling that further showers are on the way. As the front moves inland, it may produce increasingly less rain since there is less moisture in the air inland.

Coastal fog
Water in the oceans is slow to heat up, so sea fog tends to linger until the wind changes direction. Off the coast of Newfoundland, Canada (left), where warm westerly winds blow over cool currents from the Arctic, thick fogs can last for days.

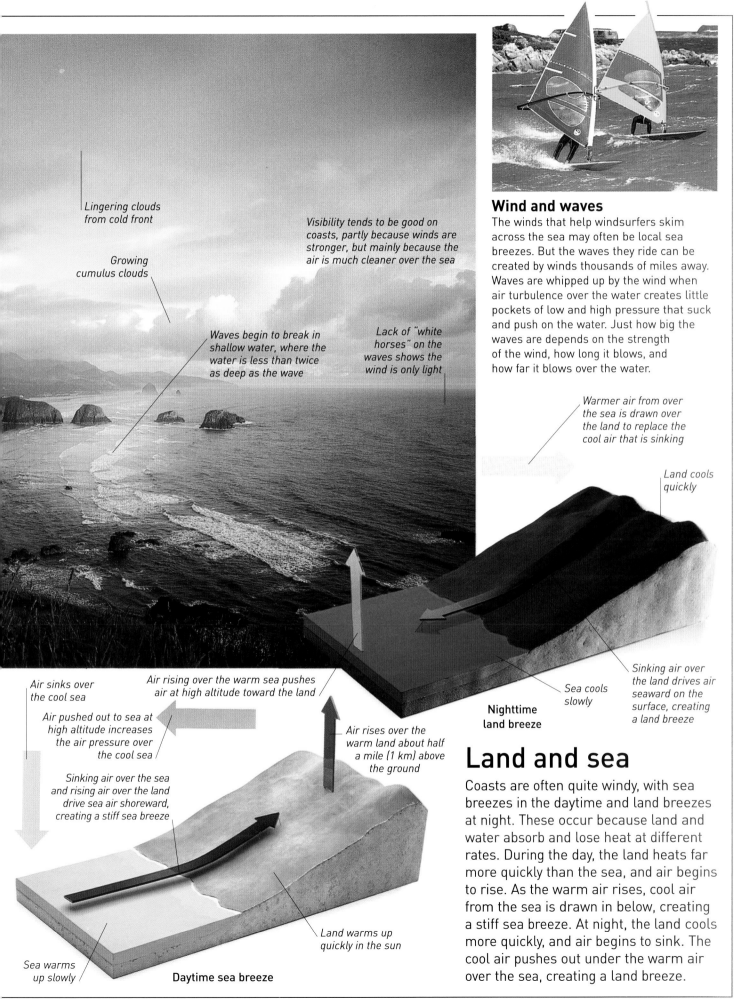

Lingering clouds from cold front

Growing cumulus clouds

Visibility tends to be good on coasts, partly because winds are stronger, but mainly because the air is much cleaner over the sea

Waves begin to break in shallow water, where the water is less than twice as deep as the wave

Lack of "white horses" on the waves shows the wind is only light

Wind and waves

The winds that help windsurfers skim across the sea may often be local sea breezes. But the waves they ride can be created by winds thousands of miles away. Waves are whipped up by the wind when air turbulence over the water creates little pockets of low and high pressure that suck and push on the water. Just how big the waves are depends on the strength of the wind, how long it blows, and how far it blows over the water.

Warmer air from over the sea is drawn over the land to replace the cool air that is sinking

Land cools quickly

Sinking air over the land drives air seaward on the surface, creating a land breeze

Sea cools slowly

Nighttime land breeze

Air sinks over the cool sea

Air rising over the warm sea pushes air at high altitude toward the land

Air pushed out to sea at high altitude increases the air pressure over the cool sea

Sinking air over the sea and rising air over the land drive sea air shoreward, creating a stiff sea breeze

Air rises over the warm land about half a mile (1 km) above the ground

Land warms up quickly in the sun

Sea warms up slowly

Daytime sea breeze

Land and sea

Coasts are often quite windy, with sea breezes in the daytime and land breezes at night. These occur because land and water absorb and lose heat at different rates. During the day, the land heats far more quickly than the sea, and air begins to rise. As the warm air rises, cool air from the sea is drawn in below, creating a stiff sea breeze. At night, the land cools more quickly, and air begins to sink. The cool air pushes out under the warm air over the sea, creating a land breeze.

Colors in the sky

Pure sunlight is white, but it is made up of the seven colors of the rainbow mixed together. As sunlight passes through the atmosphere, the colors are scattered in different directions by gases, dust, ice crystals, and water droplets. Sometimes, sunlight strikes ice and water in the air to create spectacular effects such as rainbows. These colorful arcs form in showery weather, and always appear on the opposite side of the sky to the Sun. Occasionally, electrical discharges can bring vivid color to the sky, particularly at night.

Moonbow
On rare occasions, raindrops catch the reflection of bright moonlight to form a moonbow. The colors of the moonbow are the same as those seen in a rainbow.

Polar lights
Occasionally, electrically charged particles from the Sun strike gases in the atmosphere high above the poles to create a spectacular display of colored lights in the night sky. These lights are called auroras.

Rainbow spirit
The Navajo people of southwestern US regard the rainbow as a spirit. The spirit is depicted on this blanket around two other supernatural beings, with a sacred corn plant in the center.

Low, stratus-type clouds in shadow

Saintly light

In thundery weather, sailors might see a strange, glowing ball of light on the masthead. Called "St. Elmo's Fire," this is actually an electrical discharge, like lightning.

More than one Sun

A colorful halo, or ring around the Sun is caused by ice crystals in the clouds bending sunlight. They sometimes also create bright spots, called sundogs, that look almost like other Suns.

These images are in fact the enlarged shadows of mountain climbers on clouds.

Water colors

Rainbows are sunlight that is bent and reflected by raindrops. As the light passes through a raindrop, it bends slightly. It is reflected from the back of the drop and bent again as it leaves the front. The different colors bend at different angles, which makes them separate. Red always appears at the top of the rainbow, followed by orange, yellow, green, blue, indigo, and violet.

Rainbow is created by reflection from rain in a cloud much higher in the sky

Receding cumulonimbus cloud

Red on the top, or outside, of a "primary" rainbow

Yellow in the rainbow's center

Violet on the bottom, or inside, of the rainbow

From airplanes, a rainbow can sometimes be seen as a full circle

Climate change

Since Earth's atmosphere formed around 4 billion years ago its climate has gone through many changes. One of the most dramatic changes occurred 10,000 years ago, during the last Ice Age. The weather became so cold that a third of the Earth's surface was covered in ice more than 800 ft (240 m) thick. Now, many people believe humans are changing the atmosphere so much that the world is steadily warming up, endangering our very existence.

Fossil air
As tree sap solidified into amber long ago, creatures like this spider (above) were trapped along with air bubbles.

Meteor
It is thought that the dinosaurs became extinct about 66 million years ago, when a huge meteor struck Earth, sending up so much dust that the Sun's rays were blocked out, making the planet very cold.

Preserved in ice
Ice from glaciers shows what the climate was like during the Ice Age. Bubbles of air in the ice reveal that the atmosphere contained fewer of the gases that cause global warming.

Past warmth
The world's coal and oil deposits are formed from the remains of vast forests that were growing three million years ago.

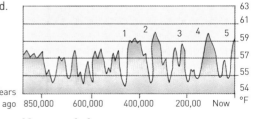

Woolly times
At the end of the last Ice Age, huge creatures, called mammoths, roamed near ice sheets far from the poles. They had long, woolly coats to protect them from the cold.

Growing evidence
Each ring in a tree trunk shows one year's growth. If rings are wide apart, the weather was warm; if close together, then the weather was cold.

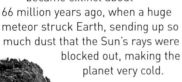

Ups and downs
Peaks in temperature over the past 850,000 years show five major warm periods (1–5 on diagram), followed by five ice ages, when temperatures on Earth were 5°F (3°C) cooler than they are now.

Viking voyage

Between 1000 and 1200 CE, the world's weather became so warm that much of the Arctic ice cap melted. At that time, Viking voyagers were sailing across the Atlantic, settling in Iceland and Greenland, and even reaching America. But between 1450–1850, during the little Ice Age, the cold weather returned, destroying Viking communities.

Diaries

Old diaries are rich sources of information on past climates. Among the best were the diaries of Thomas Barker in England between 1736–98. His journals (right) give a record of the weather over a period of more than 60 years.

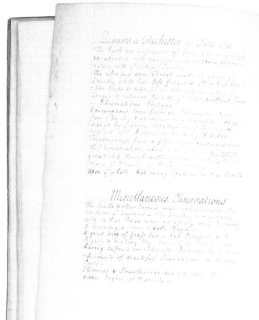

Hole in the sky

Ozone is a bluish gas high in the atmosphere that helps to protect us from the Sun's harmful ultraviolet rays. Recently, a hole has appeared in the ozone layer over the Antarctic—shown in this satellite photograph (right)—and ozone levels have declined. The chemicals causing the damage are being phased out and ozone levels have begun to recover.

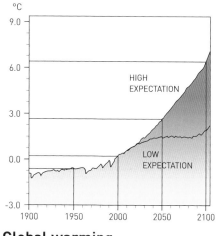

Global warming

Most meteorologists predict the world will warm between 2.7–8.6°F (1.5 and 4.8°C) by the year 2100, unless we take action now.

Satanic mills

In the early 19th century, smoke from thousands of factory chimneys and soot from millions of coal fires in homes created a real problem of smog—a mix of fog and smoke.

Climate in crisis

In recent years, people have become concerned about the effects of human activity on the world's weather. Most meteorologists believe that the world is getting warmer due to increased greenhouse gases in the atmosphere. Greenhouse gases trap heat and keep Earth warm, like the panes of glass in a greenhouse. But it is now thought that these gases are keeping Earth too warm. Carbon dioxide is the main greenhouse gas, but harmful chemicals from aerosol sprays and refrigerators also contribute to the greenhouse effect. If Earth becomes just a few degrees warmer, some places will become drier, making farming more difficult and endangering wildlife.

The death of the forest

Every year tropical forests equivalent to the size of Iceland are cut and burned to make temporary cattle pasture. Forests are made largely from carbon. If they are cleared and burned without being replaced, the carbon is released into the air as carbon dioxide—one of the main greenhouse gases that contribute to global warming.

The culprit

Car and truck exhausts release all kinds of pollutants, including vast quantities of carbon dioxide.

Home weather station

Professional meteorologists have a great deal of sophisticated equipment and thousands of weather stations to help them track the weather. But you can easily keep your own weather watch using simple instruments at home. The main thing is that you take your readings at exactly the same time at least once every day. The most important readings are rainfall, temperature, wind speed and direction, and air pressure, but you could also record cloud cover, soil temperature, and humidity.

High winds
Professional meteorologists have always tried to mount instruments for measuring wind speeds on special masts or high buildings.

Protractor

15 mph (25 kph)

0 mph (0 kph)

6 mph (10 kph)

30 mph (50 kph)

Cotton thread

Ping-Pong ball

Homemade wind gauge

Ventimeter

Air pressure in millibars

Air pressure in pounds per square inch

Moving pointer indicating pressure

Pointer to indicate lowest pressure reached

Wind speed
You can make a wind gauge using a Ping-Pong ball tied to the center of a protractor. Hold the protractor parallel to the wind so the ball is blown sideways. By reading the angle of the thread on the protractor, you can estimate the strength of the wind. A ventimeter (above) is much more accurate, but more expensive.

An aneroid barometer has a face like a clock

Air pressure
Barometers are expensive, but if you have one at home you can use it to predict the weather. A drop in air pressure indicates storms, while a rise in pressure signals good weather.

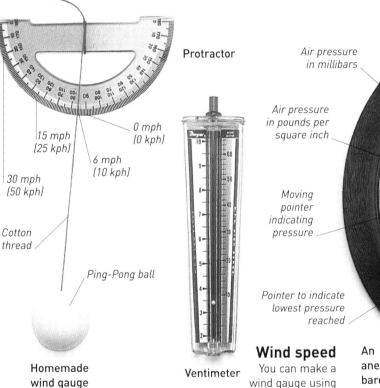

Wind direction
You can make a wind vane from balsa wood and a dowel pole. Make sure the vane's head is smaller than its tail and use a compass to work out exactly where north and south are.

A bead ensures that the vane rotates easily

Arrowhead shows the direction the wind is blowing from

N

Dowel pole

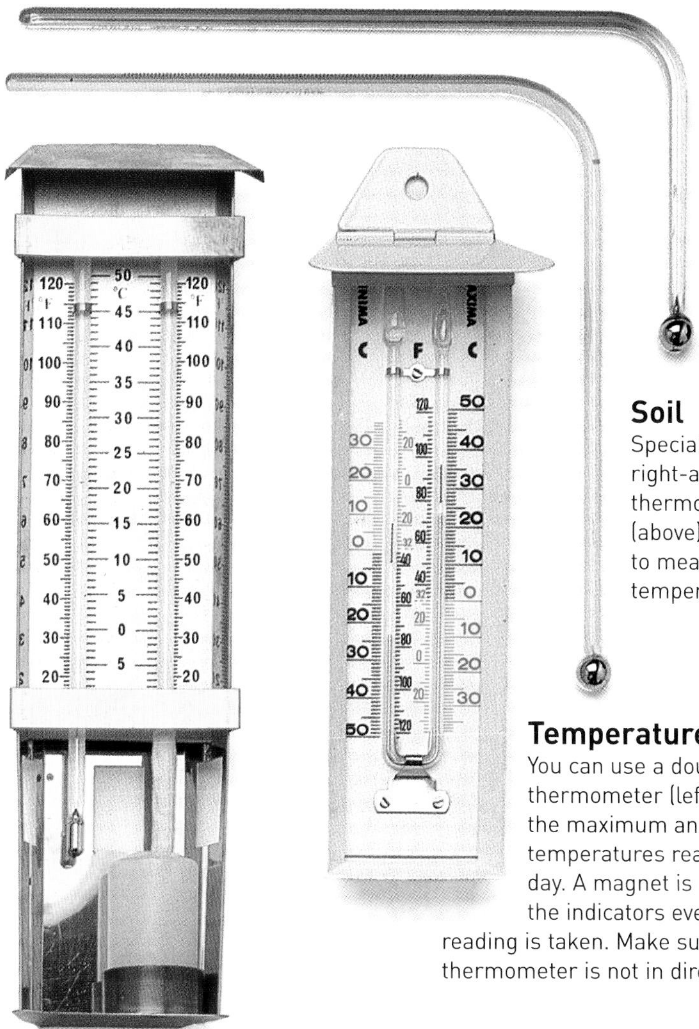

Cloud snaps
Photographs provide a visual record of weather conditions. Make a note of the exact time and date when the photo was taken.

Soil
Special, right-angled thermometers (above) are used to measure soil temperature.

Temperature range
You can use a double-ended thermometer (left) to record the maximum and minimum temperatures reached each day. A magnet is used to reset the indicators every time a reading is taken. Make sure the thermometer is not in direct sunlight.

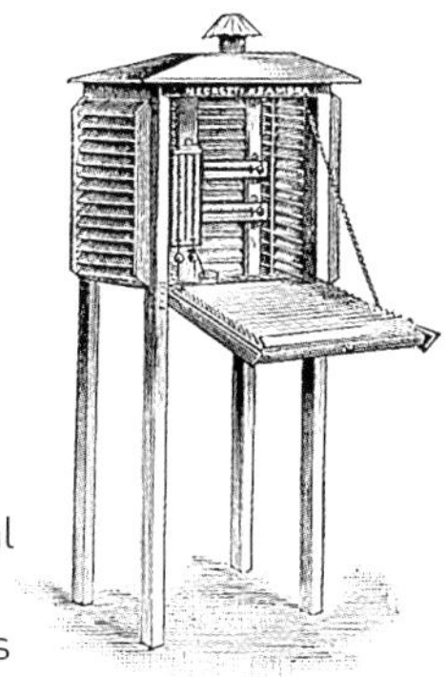

Rainfall
A plastic rain gauge is quite accurate, as long as you set it up securely at ground level in an exposed place. Take out the measuring cylinder each day to make a reading. Remember to empty it, and dry it thoroughly.

Rain gauge

Humidity
A wet and dry hygrometer (above left) has two thermometers: one bulb is wet, the other dry. The difference in temperature between them indicates the level of humidity.

Readings must be taken at the same time each day, even in heavy rain.

Sketches
Drawing clouds is a good way of learning to tell one type from another.

Screens
Professional weather instruments are kept inside ventilated shelters (above) to protect them from direct sunlight.

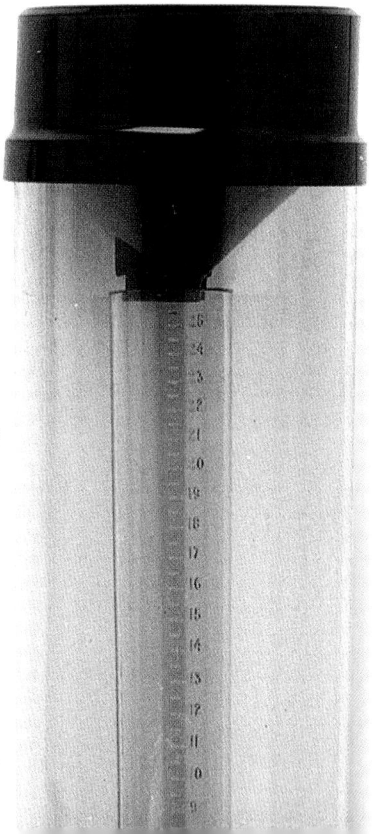

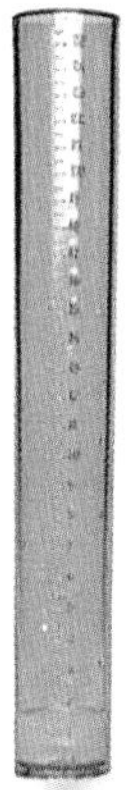

Measuring cylinder

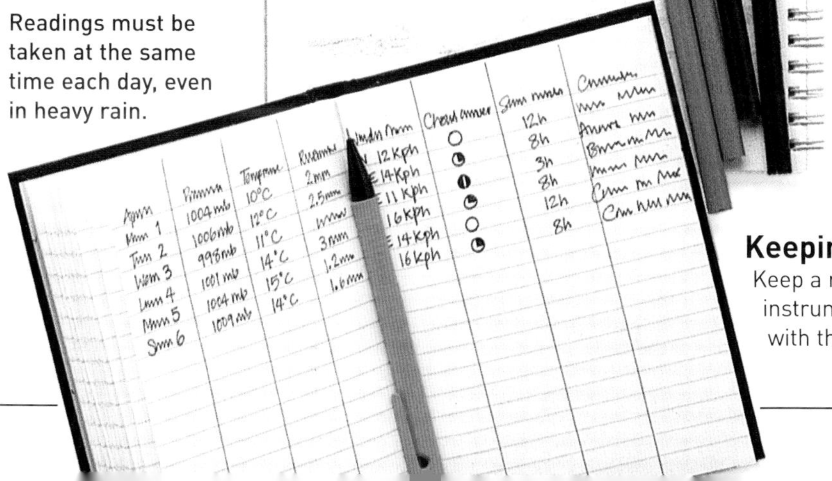

Keeping records
Keep a record of all instrument readings, with the date and time.

Did you know?

AMAZING FACTS

⚡ In very cold winters, waterfalls sometimes freeze over. Ice grows out from the side of a waterfall as splashed drops of water freeze, one on top of the other.

Frozen waterfall in the Zanskar Range, Himalaya Mountains, India

⚡ The atmosphere contains 1½ billion cubic miles (2.4 billion cubic km) of air and about 34 trillion gallons (15,470 trillion liters) of water. Because of gravity, 80 percent of the air and nearly all the moisture are in the troposphere, the part of the atmosphere closest to Earth.

⚡ Sunbathing can be dangerous even on cloudy days. The clouds reflect so much ultraviolet light from the Sun that they increase the amount of harmful rays that reach the ground, increasing the risk of skin cancer.

⚡ Very hot weather can kill. If it is too hot or humid for people's sweat to evaporate and cool them down, they get heatstroke. This can lead to collapse, coma, or even death.

⚡ The biggest desert in the world is Antarctica. It only has about 5 in (127 mm) of precipitation (snow or rain) a year, just a little more than the Sahara Desert.

⚡ It can snow in the desert. In winter, snow sometimes falls in cold deserts, such as the Great Basin in the US and the Gobi in Asia.

⚡ In 1939, hundreds of frogs fell from the sky during a storm in England. They had probably been sucked up from ponds and rivers by small tornadoes, then dropped to the ground again with the rain.

⚡ A staggering 110 million gallons (500 million liters) of rain can fall from a single thunderstorm.

Raining frog

⚡ Many reported sightings of UFOs have turned out to be lenticular clouds. Waves of wind around mountain tops form rounded clouds like flying saucers that hover motionless for hours.

Lenticular cloud

⚡ Hailstones sometimes grow to enormous size. The largest known hailstone in the world fell on Vivian, South Dakota, in 2010 and had a diameter of 8 in (20 cm). The heaviest one on record (2¼ lb/ 1 kg) fell on Bangladesh in 1986.

⚡ Trees in forests around the world are being destroyed by acid rain. Acid rain forms when pollutants from factories and cars react with sunlight and water vapor in the clouds to form sulfuric and nitric acids. These contaminate water supplies and damage forests and crops.

⚡ The average cloud only lasts for about 10 minutes.

Conifers destroyed by acid rain

QUESTIONS AND ANSWERS

Q Why does the weather keep changing all the time?

A Heat from the Sun keeps the air in motion. The Sun's power to heat the air varies, depending on its height in the sky. These variations cause the weather to change constantly.

Q What makes the wind blow?

A Winds occur wherever there are differences in air temperature and pressure. They blow from areas of high pressure to areas of low pressure.

Solar corona

Q Why are there sometimes colored rings around the Sun?

A A solar corona appears when the Sun is covered by a layer of cloud. Water droplets in the cloud split the sunlight, creating a rainbow effect.

Q What makes a large, bright disk around the moon?

A A lunar corona occurs when sunlight reflected from the moon passes through water droplets in cloud.

Earth pillars in Alberta, Canada

Q How has the weather made desert rocks such strange shapes?

A Over time, rocks are worn away by weather. Temperature changes and water make rocks crack and shatter. Also, windblown sand wears away softer rock, leaving strange shapes, such as pillars and arches.

Q Why are some deserts hot in the day and freezing at night?

A Above hot deserts, the skies are clear. The ground becomes baking hot by day since there are no clouds to shield it from the Sun, but it turns cold at night because there is nothing to trap the heat from rising up into the atmosphere.

Q How big do the biggest clouds grow?

A The biggest clouds are cumulonimbus, the big, dark rain clouds that produce thunderstorms. They can be up to 6 miles (10 km) high and hold half a million tons of water.

Desert mirage

Q What is a mirage and where do they appear?

A Mirages are tricks of the light created by very hot air. Air close to the ground is much hotter than the air above it, and light bends as it passes from one temperature to the other. This creates a shimmering reflection that looks like water. Deserts are renowned for producing mirages that look like oases.

Q How powerful is the average thunderstorm?

A A typical thunderstorm, about half a mile (1 km) across, has about the same amount of energy as 10 atom bombs.

Q When is the best time to see a rainbow?

A The best rainbows often appear in the morning or late afternoon, when the Sun is out and rain is falling in the distance. Stand with your back to the Sun and look toward the rain to see the rainbow.

Record Breakers

❄ **THE COLDEST PLACE:**
The lowest temperature recorded in the world is -128.6°F (-89.2°C) at Vostok Station, Antarctica, on July 21, 1983.

❄ **THE HOTTEST PLACE:**
At Death Valley, California, the temperature reached a record high of 134°F (56.7°C) on July 10, 1913.

❄ **THE DRIEST PLACE:**
María Elena South in Chile's Atacama Desert is the driest recorded place on Earth, with a relative humidity in the soil as low as that on Mars.

❄ **THE WETTEST PLACE:**
Mawsynram in India is the wettest place in the world, receiving an average annual rainfall of 467 in (1,187 cm).

Weather power

Many people believe that pollution from human activity is changing the climate. To reduce the amount of pollutants in the atmosphere, scientists are using the power of the weather to provide alternative, cleaner sources of energy.

La Rance tidal barrage, France

Tidal power

Energy from the tides can be converted into electricity by building a barrage across an estuary (where a river meets the sea). As the water flows in and out, it passes through machines called turbines, which generate electricity. The biggest tidal energy plant in the world crosses the La Rance estuary in France. Local weather can affect tides. Sunny skies or offshore winds can often push water away from the coastline, increasing the effects of low tides. Cloudy, rainy weather or onshore winds can push water toward the coastline, swelling high tides.

The WC-130 normally carries a crew of six people and is equipped with data-gathering instruments

US Air Force WC-130 aircraft

Hurricane hunters

A US Air Force squadron, known as the Hurricane Hunters, flies aircraft through hurricanes to monitor them and predict when and where they will hit land. The specially adapted aircraft pass through the eye (center) of the hurricane every two hours, and send back information on the hurricane's intensity and movement to the National Hurricane Center.

Tornado alley

In the US, tornadoes strike regularly in an area called Tornado Alley, between the states of South Dakota and Texas.

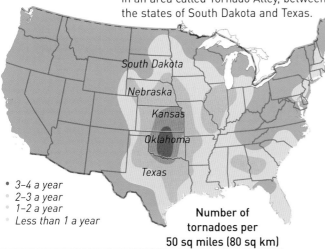

South Dakota

Nebraska

Kansas

Oklahoma

Texas

- 3–4 a year
- 2–3 a year
- 1–2 a year
- Less than 1 a year

Number of tornadoes per 50 sq miles (80 sq km)

GENERAL WEATHER WEBSITES

- An great starting point for learning about weather: **www.nws.noaa.gov/om/reachout/kidspage.shtml**

- A weather website with kid-friendly experiements: **www.eo.ucar.edu/webweather/**

- A site showing weather around the US: **www.weather.gov**

Prairie tornado photograph taken by a storm chaser

Storm chasers

Some scientists risk their lives researching tornadoes. These storm chasers use special radar equipment to look right inside storm clouds to see signs of a developing tornado.

Life in the freezer

Meteorologists based at research stations in Antarctica carry out detailed research into changing climate conditions. They also monitor the hole in the ozone layer that lies above Antarctica to find out how pollution and our efforts to prevent it are affecting the atmosphere.

Scientist launching a weather balloon into the atmosphere

Meteorologist servicing an automatic weather station

Antarctic research

In Antarctica, meteorologists carry out experiments to make long-term predictions about climate change. Other scientists study climate changes in the past and the effects of current global warming. Oceanographers and biologists research the changing ocean conditions in the icy seas around Antarctica and their effects on plant and animal life.

Each of these mirrors is computer-controlled to track the Sun across the sky during the day

Solar power

Solar power plants use thousands of wide mirrors to gather the energy from sunlight. Luz, in the Mojave Desert, in California, has the biggest solar power plant in the world. 650,000 enormous solar mirrors reflect heat onto tubes filled with oil. The hot oil heats water, which in turn makes steam. This drives turbines that generate electricity.

Wind farm near Palm Springs, California

Catching the wind

At wind farms, windmills convert the wind's energy into electricity. Wind farms only work in exposed places, and it takes about 3,000 windmills to generate as much power as a coal power plant.

Find out more

- Find out about hurricane hunters at: **www.hurricanehunters.com**

- For information on storm chases, visit: **www.stormchaser.com**

- Get information about blizzards, whiteouts, and other weather: **www.antarcticconnection.com/information/antarctic-weather/**

- Learn about weather from the National Oceanic and Atmospheric Administration: **www.pmel.noaa.gov**

- Visit a local science center to find out more about weather in your area.

Extreme weather

Weather can be violent and cause extensive damage. Every year, devastating floods, savage storms, and long periods of drought occur across the world, causing increasing concern about climate change.

STORMS AND FLOODS

Floods

Floods cause more damage than any other natural phenomenon. They swamp vast areas of dry land, destroying crops and making thousands of people homeless. In February 2000, Mozambique suffered its worst floods for 50 years, and more than a million people lost their homes.

Flood victims (left) wait to be airlifted from rooftops near Chokwe, Mozambique.

Floods at Fenton, Missouri (above)

Hurricanes

Hurricane Katrina caused devastation when it struck the Gulf Coast of the US in August 2005. More than 1,800 people died, making Katrina one of the deadliest hurricanes ever to hit the US.

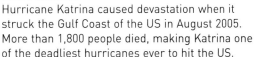

Damage from Hurricane Katrina

The Dust Bowl

In the 1930s, the American Midwest had no rain for five years, and thousands of acres of land were turned into a desert known as the Dust Bowl. Hot winds caused suffocating dust storms, and about 5,000 people died from heatstroke and breathing problems.

FIRE, SNOW, AND LANDSLIDES

The eruption of Mount St. Helens, Washington

Volcanic weather
Large volcanic eruptions affect global weather. When Mount St. Helens erupted in 1980, the entire top of the mountain blew off. Ash from the volcano was carried by high winds all around the planet, leading to hazy skies, amazing sunsets, and a brief drop in temperature.

Wildfire
Raging forest fires often start when lightning strikes vegetation during a long, dry period. On February 16, 1983, a searing heatwave in Australia triggered hundreds of forest fires. The fires spread at terrifying speed, engulfing a town, killing 70 people, and damaging vast areas of land.

Avalanches
When heavy snow builds up on a steep slope, even a small vibration can set off an avalanche. In Austria, in 1999, a block of snow weighing 170,000 tons crashed down on the village of Galtür, killing more than 30 people.

Rescuers using poles to search for victims of the Austrian avalanche

Avalanche on Mount McKinley, Alaska

Mudslides
In December 1999, 10,000 people were killed in Venezuela by devastating floods and huge mudslides. Torrential rain soaked into the hillsides creating fast-moving rivers of mud and debris, which destroyed all buildings, roads, and trees in their path.

Mudslides at La Guaira, Venezuela

Glossary

AIR MASS
A large body of air covering much of a continent or ocean, in which the temperature, pressure, and humidity are fairly constant.

AIR PRESSURE
The force of air pressing down on the ground or any other horizontal surface. Also known as atmospheric pressure.

ANEMOMETER
An instrument for measuring wind speed.

ANTICYCLONE
Also known as a "high," this is a body of air in which the air pressure is higher than it is in the surrounding air.

ATMOSPHERE
The layer of gases surrounding Earth, stretching about 600 miles (1,000 km) into space.

AURORA
Bands of colored light in the night sky. In the northern hemisphere these are called the northern lights (*aurora borealis*); in the southern hemisphere, they are called the southern lights (*aurora australis*).

Anemometer

Barograph

BAROGRAPH
An instrument that provides a continuous record of air pressure on a strip of paper wound around a revolving drum.

BAROMETER
An instrument for measuring air pressure.

BLIZZARD
A wind storm in which snow is blown into the air by very strong winds.

CIRRUS
Feathery cloud that forms at high altitudes, where the air is very cold.

CLIMATE
The normal pattern of weather in a particular place or region, averaged over a long period of time.

CLOUDS
Masses of condensed water vapor and ice particles. There are three basic cloud forms: cumulus, stratus, and cirrus.

COLD FRONT
The boundary line between warm and cold air masses, with the cold air moving toward the area of warm air in front of it.

CONDENSATION
The change from a gas, such as water vapor, to a liquid, such as water.

CORIOLIS EFFECT
The effect caused by Earth's spin, which makes winds and currents follow a curved path across the planet's surface.

CUMULONIMBUS
A cloud that produces heavy showers and thunderstorms.

CUMULUS
A large, fluffy cloud with a flat base and rounded top.

CYCLONE
A body of air in which the air pressure is lower than it is in the surrounding air. Also known as a "low."

DEPRESSION
A weather system with a centre of low pressure. It usually brings bad weather.

DEW
Moisture in the air that has condensed on objects at or near Earth's surface.

DEW POINT
The temperature at which water vapor in the air will condense.

DRIZZLE
Light rain made of drops that are smaller than 0.02 in (0.5 mm) across.

FOG
Water that has condensed from water vapor into tiny droplets near the ground, reducing visibility to less than 1,100 yd (1,000 m).

FRONT
The boundary between two air masses.

FROST
White ice crystals that form on cold surfaces when moisture in the air freezes.

GALE
A strong wind that blows at 32–63 mph (52–102 kph).

GLOBAL WARMING
A long-term increase in the atmosphere's temperature, probably caused by the greenhouse effect.

GREENHOUSE EFFECT
The warming up of Earth's surface, caused by heat from the Sun being trapped by gases in the lower atmosphere.

Hygrometer

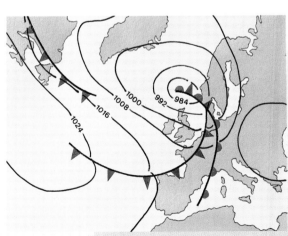

Weather chart showing fronts and isobars

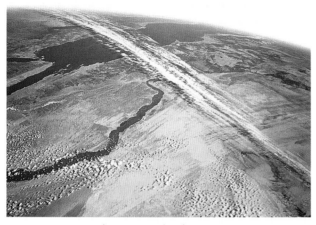
Jet stream clouds

ISOBAR
A line on a weather map that joins places with the same air pressure.

JET STREAM
A band of very strong winds in the upper atmosphere.

LIGHTNING
A discharge of static electricity from a cloud. Sheet lightning occurs within a cloud. Fork lightning occurs between a cloud and the ground.

SMOG
Originally fog mixed with smoke, but now more commonly a haze that forms in polluted air in strong sunshine.

SNOW
Ice crystals that fall from clouds and stick together to form snowflakes.

STORM
Strong winds, between gale and hurricane force, of 64–75 mph (103–121 kph).

STRATOSPHERE
The layer of Earth's atmosphere above the troposphere.

HAIL
Pellets of ice that fall from clouds.

HEMISPHERE
Half of Earth. There are northern and southern hemispheres.

HOAR FROST
Spikes of frost that form when the air is about 32°F (0°C) and water vapor touches the surfaces of trees.

HUMIDITY
The amount of water vapor in the air.

HURRICANE
A tropical cyclone that occurs in the Caribbean and North Atlantic with winds of over 75 mph (121 kph).

HYGROMETER
An instrument used for measuring humidity.

METEOROLOGY
The scientific study of weather.

MILLIBAR
The unit used to measure atmospheric pressure.

MONSOON
A wind that brings alternate wet and dry seasons to India and Southeast Asia.

OZONE LAYER
A thin layer of ozone gas in the upper atmosphere that filters out harmful ultraviolet rays from the Sun.

STRATUS
A vast, dull type of low-level cloud that forms in layers.

SYNOPTIC CHART
A weather chart that gives detailed information about conditions over a large area.

THERMAL
A rising current of warm air.

THERMOSPHERE
The top layer of the atmosphere, above about 55 miles (90 km).

Sunshine recorder

THUNDER
The sound made by expanding air during a flash of lightning.

PRECIPITATION
All forms of water that fall to the ground or form on or near it, such as rain, snow, dew, and fog.

PREVAILING WIND
The main direction from which the wind blows in a certain place.

RADIOSONDE
A package of instruments attached to a weather balloon that sends data back to Earth.

RAIN GAUGE
An instrument used to collect and measure rainfall.

RAIN SHADOW
An area of lower rainfall on the lee (sheltered) side of a hill or mountain.

TORNADO
A narrow spiral of air rotating at high speed around an area of extremely low air pressure. Wind speeds may be higher than 200 mph (320 kph).

TROPOSPHERE
The lowest or innermost layer of Earth's atmosphere, where most of the weather takes place.

TYPHOON
A tropical cyclone that occurs over the Pacific Ocean.

WARM FRONT
A boundary line between two air masses where the air behind the front is warmer than the air ahead of it.

WATERSPOUT
A column of rapidly spiralling air that forms over warm and usually shallow water, or when a tornado crosses water.

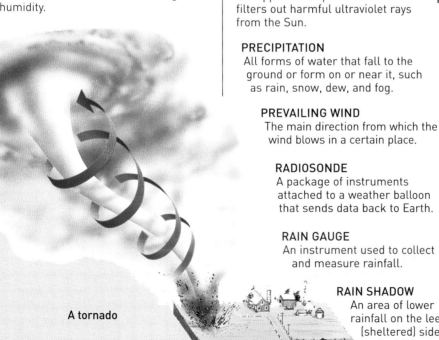
A tornado

Index

Acknowledgments

Dorling Kindersley would like to thank:
Robert Baldwin of the National Maritime
Museum, Greenwich, for making
instruments available for photography;
The Meteorological Office, Bracknell, for
providing instruments for photography;
Met Check for the loan of instruments
on pp.62–63; David Donkin for weather
models on pp.26, 34– 33, 34–35, 44–45,
and 53; Sophie Mitchell for her help
in the initial stages of the book; and
Jane Barker for the index.

For this edition, the publisher would
also like to thank: Lisa Burke for assisting
with revisions; Claire Bowers, David
Ekholm-JAlbum, Sunita Gahir, Joanne
Little, Nigel Ritchie, Susan St Louis, Carey
Scott, & Bulent Yusuf for the clipart; David
Ball, Neville Graham, Rose Horridge,
Joanne Little, & Sue Nicholson for the
wallchart; BCP, Marianne Petrou, & Owen
Peyton Jones for checking the digitized
files; Charvi Arora for editorial help,
Hazel Beynon for text editing, and Polly
Goodman for proofreading.

The publisher would like to thank the
following for their kind permission to
reproduce their images:

Picture credits:
a-above; b-below; c-center; f-far; l-left;
r-right; t=top; m=middle

Alison Anholt-White: 19, 28bc, 42cr.
Aviation Picture Library: 20cl. Bridgeman
Art Library: 17t, 42tl, 42bl, 43tr, 43br.
British Antarctic Survey: 60c. Bruce
Coleman Picture Library: 8cl, 14cr, 20c,
28tr, 28–29c, 29tl, 52b, 54bl, 54–55, 59tc.
Corbis: Tony Arruza 68bl; Bettmann 68tr;
Gary Braasch 69tl; John H. Clark 66c;
Philip James Corwin 67bl; Graham Neden/
Ecoscene 67tl, 67tr; Jim Richardson 68br;
Kevin Schafer 67cb. B. Cosgrove: 24–25,
24c, 24cr, 24bl, 25tr, 25cl, 28cl, 28c, 29tr,
29ctr, 29cr, 29cbr, 29br, Benjamin Lowy
68bl. Daily Telegraph Color Library: 7tr,
43tc. Dr. E. K. Degginer: 46cl, 46cr, 47tr,
47c, 47b. E. T. Archive: 12c, 21bl, 31br,
36tr. European Space Agency: 13tr. Mary
Evans Picture Library: 10bc, 13bl, 20tl,
24tr, 30tl, 30bl, 37tr, 41br, 44tl, 45br, 46bl,
47tl, 48b, 53cr, 54cl, 60cl, 60cr. Courtesy
of FAAM: BAE Systems Regional Aircraft
12-13ca; With thanks to Maureen Smith
and the Met Office UK. Photo by Doug
Anderson 13cr. Werner Forman Archive:
18cl, 36bl, 38c, 58b, 61tl. Courtesy of Kate
Fox: 22b. Hulton Deutsch Collection: 55br.
Hutchison Library: 31bl, 61bl. Image
Bank/ Getty Images: 43cr, 56–57, 57tr,
66br. Istituto e Museo di Storia della
Scienza (photos Franca Principe): 2br, 3bl,
10bl, 10r, 11tl, 11c, 11r, 11b. Landscape
Only: 23cr. Frank Lane Picture Library:
20bl, 22tl, 30c, 36c, 41bl, 44bl. Mansell
Collection: 18tl 43cbl, 43cl.Meteorological
Office: 12bl, 12br © Crown, 14cl, 15tl,
21t, 34t, 42tr, 45tl, 45tcl, 45c, 45tcr, 45tr,
49bl. N.A.S.A.: 16tl. National Center
for Atmospheric Research: 13br, 37tc.
N.H.P.A.: 44cl. R.K.Pilsbury: 8crt, 8crb,
15tc, 26–27, 32cl, 33lt, 33c, 34cl, 34bl, 35t,
50cl, 50c, 50cl, 51ct, 51tl, 51bl. Planet
Earth: 9cl, 18cr, 20br, 23cl, 41t, 53tr,
54br, 55bl, 56b. Popperfoto: 21bl, Peter
Andrews/ Reuters 68cl; Andy Mettler/
Reuters 69cr; Kimberly White/Reuters
69br. Rex Features: 13tl. Ann Ronan
Picture Library: 6tl, 12t, 13cl, 14tl, 23bl,
27bl, 27br, 38tl, 61cr. Royal Meteorological
Society: 28tl. David Sands: 25br. M.
Saunders: 20–21t Scala: 11tc. Science
Photo Library: 36–37, 40c, 40bl, 40bc,
58c, 58–59, 61cl, Simon Fraser 64cl, 64br;
Damien Lovegrove 65bl; Magrath/Folsom
64tr; David Nunuk 65tc; Pekka Parviainen
65cl. Frank Spooner/Gamma: 38bl. Stock
Boston: 48c. Tony Stone Picture Library:
6bl, 18bl, 31t, 48–49, 52–53. Wildlife
Matters: 8tr, 9tr. Zefa: 7cb, 7b, 24cl,
25tl, 39t, 47tc, 49br, 50bl, 61br.

Illustrations: Eugene Fleury, John
Woodcock

All other images © Dorling Kindersley

For further information see:
www.dkimages.com